Understanding a Changing World

UNDERSTANDING A CHANGING WORLD

The Alternative Futures of the International System

DONALD R. KELLEY

ROWMAN & LITTLEFIELD
Lanham • Boulder • New York • London

Published by Rowman & Littlefield
An imprint of The Rowman & Littlefield Publishing Group, Inc.
4501 Forbes Boulevard, Suite 200, Lanham, Maryland 20706
www.rowman.com

6 Tinworth Street, London SE11 5AL, United Kingdom

British Library Cataloguing in Publication Information Available

Library of Congress Cataloging-in-Publication Data
Names: Kelley, Donald R., 1943– author.
Title: Understanding a changing world : the alternative futures of the international system / Donald R. Kelley.
Description: Lanham, Maryland : Rowman & Littlefield, 2021. | Includes bibliographical references and index.
Identifiers: LCCN 2020045280 (print) | LCCN 2020045281 (ebook) | ISBN 9781538127933 (cloth) | ISBN 9781538127940 (paperback) | ISBN 9781538127957 (epub)
Subjects: LCSH: International relations. | International economic relations. | World politics—21st century.
Classification: LCC JZ1242 .K46 2021 (print) | LCC JZ1242 (ebook) | DDC 327—dc23
LC record available at https://lccn.loc.gov/2020045280
LC ebook record available at https://lccn.loc.gov/2020045281

♾️™ The paper used in this publication meets the minimum requirements of American National Standard for Information Sciences—Permanence of Paper for Printed Library Materials, ANSI/NISO Z39.48-1992.

For Cole Alex Ogden

Contents

Understanding a Changing World

The Future(s) of the International System

WHY FUTURE(S)?

The use of the plural "futures" is intentional. We live in a changing world, and the possible futures before us are increasingly complex. The once seemingly predictable road ahead now forks in new and uncertain directions. The widely accepted certainties that spoke of globalization and interdependence, the spread of democracy in a succession of "waves" or "springs," and a post–Cold War reduction of conflict now are open to reinterpretation. Economic, social, and political changes roil nations, regional blocs, and the very nature of the international system. The path(s) ahead are far less certain, as is our confidence in how we should interpret and teach them.

Why be concerned? The future is coming, one way or another, and we are going to have to deal with it. In the past, such fatalistic uncertainty has been the exception rather than the rule. Driven by the disorder of the world around us, and guided by whatever our institutions, cultures, or ideologies told us about how things should be, we crafted a number of international systems designed to meet the needs of the day, or perhaps merely to institutionalize a new status quo to reflect current reality. Whatever their origins, these international systems attempted to create institutions and rules that told us how the actors on the international stage should interact. Sometimes they were essentially descriptive: This is the way things are, like it or not. Power is not evenly distributed among the states or other actors, and that reality shapes the system within which we must live. Sometimes they were prescriptive: This is the way things should be, especially if we want to reach certain goals like political stability, economic growth, or social development. If that's the case, here are the things we must change to advance toward that goal. Sometimes they were a product of a system-defining international conference (the Treaty of Westphalia, the Congress of Vienna, or the Versailles Conference, for example), and sometimes their origin was less clearly defined (the Atlantic Charter, the Bretton Woods Conference, or the United Nations conference in San Francisco, each setting forth a part of what was supposed to be the post–World War II world). And sometimes they simply fell into place in the face of unexpected events (the Cold War modifications to the expected post–World War II arrangements, and the eventual end of the Cold War). Most often they were a mixture of all of the above.

Students of international relations know these systems by familiar names: the Westphalian system; the balance of power; collective security; hegemonic, bipolar, or multipolar systems; or perhaps merely as historical periods like the Cold War or the post–Cold War world. Such designations are useful bits of conventional wisdom. In general terms, they tell us who the actors are, how they are arranged on the playing field, and how the game is played. And they tell us where we fit in. But they also leave out a lot, especially what comes next, because these systems are never completely stable. Created at some turning point in history—usually after a particularly disruptive war or some other systemic malfunction—they attempt to diagnose why the previous system failed and how we should reassemble the pieces. At their core, they are artificial constructs of a new world order, designed by those who best survived the disintegration of the old order and had a stake in the defining the future.

What Is an International System?

An international system is an artificial construct, a set of ideas, concepts, and relationships that tells us how the world is structured and how it works. Later, we'll call the various versions of the international systems that have emerged since the Treaty of Westphalia in 1648 by a much fancier name—paradigms—because our notions of how these systems operate play a central role in setting the international stage. Like paradigms in the sciences, they become the central ordering principles that set forth our core beliefs and expectations—at least until they no longer seem adequate, and then they must change or be abandoned. In the sciences, the older paradigms that told us that the earth was the center of the solar system or that all things were made up of a combination of earth, fire, air, and water failed in the face of increasingly sophisticated knowledge, and something new had to replace them. Eventually scientists got used to the idea. A part of scientific process always had to be about testing the conventional wisdom of the day, producing either confirmation or growing evidence that eventually a "paradigm shift" might be necessary. It was more complicated in the social sciences, in which paradigms were less precisely defined and the criteria of confirmation or rejection less clear. But sometimes it happened: the nineteenth-century balance-of-power system failed to keep the peace in Europe, or the first version of collective security institutionalized in the ill-fated League of Nations produced neither collective action nor security.

Accepting the reality that paradigms change over time brings us no closer to a working definition of an international system as a paradigm. One leading textbook in international relations refers to it as "a set of interacting elements" seen primarily in terms of the number of the "elements" and the "global distribution of wealth and technological development."[1] The definition of "international system" offered by the *Encyclopedia Britannica* points us to a number of important elements, including the "structure of the system," "interaction between the units," the formal and informal "rules" and "norms" that govern their interaction, and "the implications for war and peace, cooperation or conflict, and the existence of different types of states."[2] "Structure" refers to the overall configuration of the system. Is it unipolar, dominated by a single hegemon with exceptional power and responsibility? Is it bipolar, with power distributed between two powerful nations or blocs? Or is it multipolar, with power and influence distributed among a number of entities? "Interaction between the units" raises two other important questions. What are the "units"? Are they mostly nation-states in the conventional Westphalian sense, or is the picture more complex, including international organizations (sovereign states joined in a body such as the United Nations), supranational bodies (to which states surrender a portion of their sovereignty, such as the European Union [EU]), non-state actors (for example, multinational corporations, international civil society, or other entities aspiring to be but not yet fully recognized as states)? Equally important is the second element: How do these "units," however defined, interact? Bilaterally? Multilaterally? Are they equal, or are some more equal than others? What are the "rules" and unwritten "norms" that shape their conduct? And finally, what are the broader implications of any particular paradigm? What will it mean in terms of outcomes as fundamental as war and peace and the nature of international society? Hedley Bull, a leading British scholar, expands the notion to include "international society." He writes that "an international system refers to a set of regularly interacting political actors that are sufficiently interdependent to make the behavior of each influential on the other. When these actors are conscious of common interests and share certain fundamental values, they can be considered members of an international society."[3]

WHAT IS A PARADIGM?

The dictionary calls a paradigm "a typical example or a pattern of something; a model" and points us toward synonyms like "template" or "prototype." For our purposes, paradigms are intellectual and conceptual frameworks that tell us how to think analytically about something—in this case, the nature of the international system and the forces that shape it.[4] The paradigms give us differing views of how international systems are structured and how they operate and the nature of the underlying forces that animate them. They tell us who the actors are; how they interact with each other, both within formal institutions and informally through ad hoc arrangements; and how these arrangements shape the world around us. Another way to understand a paradigm is to think of it as describing a game: telling us who the players are, how the teams are organized, the rules of the game, the nature of the playing field, and how the game is refereed and scored.

For paradigms to work in the real world, they must be translated into operational concepts, action plans, and institutions. The success or failure of the paradigm per se is linked to the success or failure of these institutions, whether it be the Westphalian nation-state, the balance of power, or the mechanisms of collective security embodied in the League of Nations or the United Nations.

Paradigms often have significant political meaning. Janus-like, they simultaneously look to the past and to the future. How did we get to this point in history, and what should be preserved and what should be transformed in the new order we hope to build? Such paradigms are frequently at the core of political movements that promise to build that better world, and that promise is a central element of their claim to legitimacy and purpose. Paradigms evoke passion, commitment, and loyalty as well as condemnation, rejection, and loathing. While each has its own philosophical and institutional underpinnings, each also faces its own version of political reality and expediency. Leaders must be chosen and vested with political legitimacy; institutions must be created and charged with their particular role in the new world order; followers must be identified and mobilized for the coming struggle; and "truth" must be articulated and promulgated in ways that link the leaders and the led.

BUILDING ANALYTIC PARADIGMS AND ALTERNATIVE FUTURES

As the title of this book suggests, our purpose is to look ahead to the possible alternative international systems that may emerge. We are not going to try to predict exactly which of these possible futures will emerge or how they will operate down to the last detail. But what we can do is suggest the most likely possible futures and how they might evolve out of today's international order, building on the nature of the current world and, most importantly, on the ways in which we conceptualize the forces that will shape its future.

That's where analytic paradigms come in. They provide the prevailing frameworks within which we build our descriptions of possible international systems. Who are the primary and secondary participants in the system? How is the system arranged or institutionalized? What are the rules of engagement? And what are the driving forces that animate the system, leading it toward conflict or cooperation? Paradigms give us a widely accepted common model of how things work, providing a distinct set of concepts and relationships that seems to explain the world in which we live and how we are destined to interact with it. They provide the conventional wisdom of the day and, if we truly accept them, an intellectual comfort level that we have figured things out.

Such paradigms also have their weaknesses. What if the conventional wisdom fails, or the commonly accepted model no longer seems to explain how things work? And what if the once commonly accepted model is challenged by new inescapable realities that no longer provide an intellectually secure comfort zone or predictable results? What if new concepts, theories, and models attract widespread support, slowly at first but then with growing speed as the old paradigm is increasingly questioned? Or what if there are competing paradigms at the same time, each seemingly offering a possible but as yet unproven version of a new conventional wisdom? In fact, this happens all the time, producing moments of uncertainty in the search for new paradigms. The rejection or substantial modification of a paradigm is called a "paradigm shift," creating a new model or template, or a new "game" with new players, rules, and outcomes.[5]

PARADIGMS IN THE SOCIAL SCIENCES

Paradigms commonly used in the social sciences usually are less precise than those in the natural sciences, making them harder to confirm or disconfirm. But their essential role and structure remain the same. They create an overall model through which we view and attempt to understand some aspect of human behavior. They give us the foundations on which we build a more comprehensive view of the world and how its elements interact. When they are broadly accepted as conventional wisdom, they give us the playbook by which we engage that world. And when they spectacularly fail, usually after a game-changing conflict or revolution, they demand that we begin again, sometimes with great confidence that we understand what has happed and what must be done, and sometimes with limited understanding of what just happened and what we should do next.

Before we discuss the dominant paradigms that have shaped the contemporary world and how they might shape its future, two important caveats are in order. First, paradigms are not the same as academic disciplines. "Economics" per se is not a paradigm. But there are a number of paradigms that are built around economic issues that shape our thinking about how the world works. Marxism, laissez-faire economics, and the "Chicago school" are just a few, and each functions as a different paradigm insofar as it answers the basic questions at the core of any paradigm: how is the system structured, who are the actors, and what are the rules of the game? In a similar fashion, the nation-state, culture, and ideology are not paradigms in the abstract. They can tell us where to look for answers, but the real paradigms don't emerge until we fill in the details. What kind of nation-state, and what is the structure of the system? Which culture, and what do its values and norms tell us about how culture shapes the international system? Or what ideology, and how does it shape our view of how the world works?

REALISM, LIBERALISM, AND CONSTRUCTIVISM: THE TRADITIONAL POINTS OF VIEW

The second caveat deals with the importance of other, more traditional paradigms that are used to describe the international system: realism, liberalism, and constructivism, and all of their variations. Each offers its own paradigm setting forth the basic nature and modus operandi of the international system. Every basic textbook pays homage to their important role, usually beginning with their evolution through a series of initial interpretations and morphing through a series of "neo-doctrines" as other scholars have modified them. Whatever their individual strengths and weaknesses, they are central to the discipline, and our current effort is in no way an attempt to deny their continuing role. It is not an intellectual debate between the "old" and the "new."[6]

That said, there are times when the conventional approaches don't seem to address the task at hand. Trying to think about the future in terms of concrete scenarios is one of those times. While realism, liberalism, and constructivism might give us some of the points of departure and start us in a particular direction, they don't give us enough details to construct complex and viable models of what those different futures might be. That's why we turn to different conceptualizations—or paradigms, as we have called them—that seem to serve our current intellectual needs. To be sure, each of these paradigms draws elements from the more traditional theories, which is one of their strengths. But they also draw elements from other intellectual frameworks, sometimes combining aspects of realism and constructivism, or liberalism and ideology, to produce configurations that are clearly discernable (or perhaps merely imaginable) in the real world. That, hopefully, is their intellectual and pragmatic usefulness.

Realism is closely identified with the current nation-state paradigm. It focuses on the structure of the international system composed of the classical Westphalian nation-state arranged into hegemonic, bipolar, or multipolar configurations. Motivated by the desire to seek power (the traditional realist interpretation) or security (the neorealist version), nation-states seek to bring order to an anarchy-prone and dangerous world in which the strong dominate the weak. While cooperation is possible in circumstances where nation-states receive "relative gains," it is a temporary respite from a world in which all players pursue their own "national interest" through "self-help" and jealously guard their ultimate sovereignty.

Despite its simplistic and sobering assessment of the structure and modus operandi of the international system, realism does little to tell us what may lie ahead. Little is said to let us know what political, economic, or cultural factors define the "national interest," much less how it may change over time. At best, we are left to conclude that the future will somehow be shaped by human nature, which is presumed to be deeply rooted in self-interest and power seeking, by the shifting strengths of the nation-states themselves or their alliances, and by the particular configuration of the international system itself.

Liberalism is most closely aligned with our economic paradigm, although it may include strong elements of identity and ideology. It focuses less on the structural features of the international system and more on a behavioral analysis of the various incentives to international cooperation, conflict avoidance, and mediation. Less pessimistic about human nature, the likelihood of anarchy, and the power-seeking motivation of people and nation-states, it is built upon the notion of rational cooperation for mutual gain at all levels, including economic well-being, shared security arrangements, and social and intellectual progress. Increasing negotiation and interaction, economic interdependence, and shared cultural values underpin a world in which the role of the traditional nation-states is guided by a growing sense of common purpose and shared fate, a reality that is further institutionalized by the growing role of non-state actors, an activist international civil society, and international norms that bridge the remaining gaps among nation-states. Liberalism stresses the importance of domestic politics within nation-states, opting for the spread of liberal pluralistic democracy and the advent of "democratic peace" among nations. In institutional terms, it envisions the transformation of the Westphalian nation-state into an instrument of greater international cooperation, less concerned with its role in managing anarchy and defending its sovereignty and more involved in the enlightened pursuit of beneficial economic, security, and social policies.

Liberalism predictably envisions the future in more complex terms than earlier realists, less dependent on structural features alone and more determined by the complex interplay of an optimistic assessment of human nature, deepening economic interdependence, the spread of democratic government, growing acceptance of international norms that mitigate conflict, and the role of an ever more complex assortment of institutional arrangements, including the new-and-improved nation-state, international and supranational bodies, and a host of non-state actors.

Constructivism defines the international system in psychological terms built around self- and group identity, in- and out-group distinctions, and a series of personal and social narratives that shape behavioral norms and institutional interactions. Simply put, identity and the institutions that embody it are social constructs, invented to impose order on the broader world and tell us where we fit in. Social, economic, and cultural elites play a key and usually self-serving role in its creation, preservation, and change, and self-appointed counter-elites emerge as its critics, enemies, and occasional replacements. Identity comes from many sources: the Westphalian sense of nationalism, tied to the traditional nation-state; the sense of cultural identity, broadly defined to include ethnicity, religion, or other distinctive cultural markers; and ideological identity, defined in terms of adherence to a particular doctrine. Identities create narratives and scripts that define reality for their adherents, establishing friends and enemies and deeply shaping the formal institutions that are created to translate identity into social action. For constructivists, therefore, any change in the international system begins with a change in the nature of core identities and social constructs.

THE FOUR PARADIGMS: THE NATION-STATE, ECONOMICS, CULTURE, AND IDEOLOGY

Since the Treaty of Westphalia, which ended the Thirty Years' War in 1648, the development of the many different paradigms that have emerged has been based on a seemingly endless debate over the significance of four different approaches around which these paradigms might be built. These are:

- **the Nation-State Paradigm,** built around the debate over the role of the traditionally defined Westphalian nation-state, and the significance of various sub- or supranational entities that might challenge its dominance;

- **the Economic Paradigm,** built around the debate over the centrality of economic issues, including the defining role of various economic theories, of various trade regimes (mercantilism, comparative advantage, globalization, interdependence, economic nationalism, etc.) and their impact on national, regional, and global economies;

- **the Identity and Culture Paradigm,** built around the debate over the centrality of culture and identity, embodied in conventional notions about national identity per se as well as other religious, ethnic, cultural, and associational identities; and

- **the Ideological Paradigm,** built around the debate over the centrality of ideology, sometimes embodied in the confrontation of conflicting ideologies (liberalism, socialism, fascism, etc.) and sometimes embodied in a broader and more nuanced debate over the definition of political and social legitimacy.

Each of these debates has given rise to many different paradigms, and the level of complexity increases as the paradigms interact. Standing alone, each paradigm offers a point of departure (the nation-state, economics, identity and culture, or ideology) and then extrapolates, within the parameters of that mindset, the alternative futures that might occur. In the real world, no one paradigm will completely command the field. The individual paradigms are internally conflicted; merely saying that economics or culture or ideology will play a significant role does not say which economic theory or culture or ideology will dominate the paradigm. Moreover, paradigms will interact and influence one another, sometimes merging into predictable combinations but sometimes morphing into unique patterns.

WHAT COMES NEXT?

If you are expecting specific predictions about the future of the international system, you are going to be disappointed. Our goal is more modest, but hopefully also more intellectually stimulating. What follows are a number of what Albert Einstein called "thought experiments," evoking the disciplined imagination of the analyst that begins with what he or she now knows and extrapolates what may happen in the future based upon the paradigm that he or she is using. Each "experiment" begins with what seem to be reasonable assumptions about the way the world is today and how it might be shaped by the dominance of one or another paradigm. If the economic paradigm emerges as the most important driving force, then it will suggest a series of future scenarios. But if culture or ideology dominate, then movement in other directions is likely. And of course, no one paradigm is likely to control all aspects of a changing international system. They will complete for the mantle of the new conventional wisdom, as they always have, sometimes standing defiantly alone, but more typically interacting and mutually influencing one another in the search for more sophisticated and nuanced interpretations.

NOTES

1. Charles Russett, Harvey Staar, and David Kinsella, *World Politics: A Menu for Choice*, 9th ed. (Wadsworth, 2020), 18–19.

2. Charles A. McClelland and Robert Pfaltzgraff, "International Relations," https://www.britannica.com/topic/international-relations; see also Karen A. Mingst and Ivan M. Arrenguin-Tuft, *Essentials of International Relations*, 7th ed. (Norton, 2017), ch. 4, "The International System," 106–31.

3. Hedley Bull, *The Anarchical Society: A Study of Order in World Politics* (Cambridge University Press, 1977), quoted in Charles W. Kegley Jr. and Gregory A. Raymond, *The Global Future: A Brief Introduction to World Politics*, 4th ed. (Wadsworth, 2012), 276–77.

4. *Merriam-Webster's Dictionary*, "Paradigm," http://www.mirriam-webster.com.

5. Thomas S. Kuhn and Ian Hacking, *The Structure of Scientific Revolutions: 50th Anniversary Edition* (University of Chicago Press, 2012).

6. For a discussion of the conventional paradigms, see Elizabeth G. Matthews and Rhonda L. Callaway, *International Relations Theory: A Primer* (Oxford University Press, 2016); Paul R. Viotti and Mark V. Kauppi, *International Relations Theory*, 5th ed. (Pearson, 2011); Tim Dunne and Milja Kurki, *International Relations Theory: Discipline and*

Diversity (Oxford University Press, 2016); Oliver Daddow, *International Relations Theory,* 3rd ed. (SAGE, 2017); and Stephanie Lawson, *Theories of International Relations: Contending Approaches to World Politics* (Polity, 2015).

2

The Nation-State Paradigm

THE PARADIGM

The nation-state paradigm holds that the role of the territorially defined post-Westphalian nation-state remains central to the structure of and interaction within the international system, although other international, supranational, or subnational entities play a role. The paradigm posits:

- **The nation-state is the primary actor in the international arena and remains the key, if not the exclusive, actor within regional blocs and international/supranational organizations.**

Created by the Treaty of Westphalia in 1648 to bring peace and order to Europe at the end of the Thirty Years' War, the nation-state was intended to change how states defined themselves and how they interacted on the international stage. With the influential role of the Holy Roman Empire and the papacy now destroyed by irresolvable religious conflict, the new system offered a combination of political and territorial arrangements, coupled with a revision of the role of diplomacy, to keep order. As Henry Kissinger puts it, "The Westphalian peace reflected a practical accommodation to reality, not a unique moral insight. It relied on a system of independent states refraining from interference in each other's domestic affairs and checking each other's ambition through a general equilibrium of power."[1]

Central to the new world order was the concept of the nation-state. It combined two different but mutually supportive characteristics: a *nation*, which was to embody a sense of common identity based on historical association, culture, language, religion, and whatever else bound a people together, and a *state*, which was a territorial, legal, and political expression of which government controlled which territory. The *nation* part was to create stable communities in which religion was only one of many defining characteristics and to give rise to a sense of national identity that bound a people together and distinguished them from others. The *state* part was to define national boundaries (admittedly subject to revision) and encourage the creation of effective central governments that could bring order within their borders and deal with other nations through diplomacy. All nation-states would be equal to one another (at least in the legal sense), possess complete sovereignty (total control of what happened within their own borders and immunity from interference from others), and enjoy territorial integrity (no other country could enter their realm). In the real world, these guarantees were less than perfect, but they did set the standard for most countries most of the time and established the concept of the nation-state as the most durable building block of the international order.

- **The nation-state maintains the claim of ultimate sovereignty, although it de facto accepts wide-ranging, although ultimately revocable, limitations.**

In a perfect Westphalian world, *sovereignty* lets any nation-state claim to have complete control over what it does within its own borders, with no other nation empowered to interfere with or entitled to pass judgment on its actions. My country, my rules . . . The legal fiction of such perfect independence is an important touchstone of diplomacy and international law. But in the real world, sovereignty is less than perfect. Sometimes it is compromised by harsh realities; a more powerful nation forces another to do its bidding. Sometimes it is voluntarily surrendered for mutual gain; nations enter into agreements or join international organizations that facilitate some common goal, like mail delivery from one country to another or exchanging information about the weather, epidemics, pollution, or global warming. Sometimes the agreements are more political. Military alliances such as the North Atlantic Treaty Organization (NATO) or the USSR-led Warsaw Pact (WTO) bind nations in common cause against an enemy, and economic pacts like the European Union or the North American Free Trade Agreement (NAFTA) (now the United States-Mexico-Canada Agreement [USMCA]) promote trade and make nations increasingly interdependent. More rarely, nations create supranational arrangements like the political institutions of the EU or the International Criminal Court, which more fundamentally compromise sovereignty. But there is always an escape clause, a way for a nation to withdraw from the arrangement and reassert control, such as the withdrawal of Great Britain from the EU or the American departure from the Paris Agreement on global warming and climate change.

- **Nation-states seek to identify and act upon a sense of "national interest," variously expressed through the domestic political process.**

First mentioned by Niccolo Machiavelli in *The Prince*, national interest includes the inherent and immutable goals of a particular state.[2] In general terms, it includes those things that all nations must seek: security, territorial integrity, sovereignty, and above all else, power. Translating those goals into more specific actions is the responsibility of the nation's leaders and the political process, which almost always means that conflicting interpretations emerge. Speaking to the House of Commons in 1848, British prime minister Lord Palmerston summed it up: "We have no permanent allies, and we have no perpetual enemies. Our interests are eternal and perpetual, and those interests it is our duty to follow."[3] While the ends would remain the same, the means would be adjusted to suit the needs of the moment, sometimes producing strange bedfellows and seemingly contradictory alliances. Nations would set aside fundamental differences in political style or culture to form alliances against a common enemy (the alliance of Britain, France, and Tsarist Russia against Germany before World War I, and a similar configuration including the United States in opposition to Nazi Germany in World War II). Alliances would shift over time, and old enemies would become friends (many of the former Eastern European communist states are now members of NATO, and Japan and the United States openly cooperate against the rise of the People's Republic of China).

Accepting the idea that a national interest exists begs the question of who is to decide what it is. The easy answer is that each nation-state has a domestic political process to make those decisions. But what if that process produces disagreement over the fundamental core interests as well as the details of their implementation? Is the illusive but reassuring sense of an immutable national interest really just the always-shifting conventional wisdom of the day? Throughout the Cold War, there was broad consensus that opposition to the spread of communism was a high priority. But there was also bitter disagreement over whether involvement in local wars in places like Vietnam or revolutions in Latin America or Africa was the best way to serve that broader interest.

- **Nation-states conceptualize the international system in terms of structural or "polar" configurations, identifying themselves and others in terms of unipolar (hegemonic), bipolar, or multipolar roles.**

Nation-states tend to see the structure of the international system and their place within it through the prism of their place within polar and hierarchical configurations; their own absolute and relative power; their self-identity, placing emphasis on the role of individual, sovereign entities; the diplomatic and institutional mechanisms through which they interact; and the overall level of order or anarchy in the system as a whole. While this sets the stage for multiple and sometimes conflicting interpretations of a nation's place in the system, it also provides for a complex and nuanced overall view of how the international system operates. For example, the end of the Cold War initially resulted in a redefinition of the international system as unipolar or limited multipolar in nature. Within that redefined context, virtually all nations had to reassess their own role within what initially seemed to be a unipolar, hegemonic world with the United States as the most powerful actor. With time, that initial perception gradually morphed into a redefined and far more complex multipolar world, shaped by the growing economic and military power of China, the reemergence of the Russian Federation, and the American temptation to diminish its global role. Yet other changes also made their mark: growing disorder within the European Union; Great Britain's Brexit decision to leave the EU; growing opposition to the economic integration and globalization that had underpinned a post–World War II consensus on how to bring order to the international system; and the emergence of both right- and left-wing populism in Europe and the United States that undercut long-standing centrist governments. Other fundamental changes also forced a reconsideration of conventional wisdom: the growing salience and controversial nature of issues like global warming and environmental degradation; the reemergence of long-dormant economic disputes over the concentration of wealth and economic power within and among nations and between the relatively more prosperous northern hemisphere and the less developed southern hemisphere; and the accelerating impact of new technologies in global communications, artificial intelligence, and weaponry. The important point is that the analysts and practitioners who accept the nation-state paradigm tend to view all of these developments through the prism of the traditional Westphalian state, perhaps updated and modernized a bit, but still essentially the same. Changes of the basic structure of the international system are still defined essentially in terms of the relative capabilities and hierarchical rearrangement of nation-states, with international or supranational entities playing a secondary role. No surprises there, at least to the proponents of the nation-state-centered worldview. The future will be a product of the interplay of elements with which we are already familiar, creating a sort of intellectual "comfort zone" in a changing world. To be sure, complexities and uncertainties abound, requiring discipline and sophistication from the analyst, and a high tolerance for ambiguity and a nuanced view of the international system. From the beginning, the nation-state system has "processed" similar changes, and there is no reason to assume that it cannot do so again.

THE POSSIBLE FUTURES

When viewed from the perspective of a nation-state-centered international system, several possible alternative futures emerge (see table 2.1). They include:

- **a hegemonic system,** built around the dominance of a single dominant state;
- **a new balance of power system,** built around a bipolar or limited multipolar world;
- **a stable multipolar world,** built around the interaction of a growing number of powerful nations; and
- **an increasingly unstable multipolar system,** built around increasingly dysfunctional states within an increasingly dysfunctional international system.

A HEGEMONIC WORLD

The Structure of a Hegemonic World

A hegemonic world is one in which a single overwhelmingly powerful nation-state dominates a clearly defined and hierarchical international system. The hegemon is accepted or perhaps just grudgingly acknowledged as the dominant state, whose influence and power shape the world.

Table 2.1. The Nation-State Paradigm

Hegemonic World	Balance of Power in a Bipolar or Limited Multipolar World	Stable Multipolar World	Unstable Multipolar World
Dominant nation with military, economic, and "soft" power	System dominated by a handful of major powers	Increasingly complex multipolar structure	Unstable hierarchy among 1st-, 2nd-, and 3rd-tier nations
Voluntarily exercises proactive and reactive leadership	All seek to prevent the emergence of a hegemon	Economic and military power more widely dispersed	Increasing political instability within nations in all tiers
Dominates agenda and goal setting	Limited number of 2nd- and 3rd-tier nations increasingly influence the system	First-tier nations find it more difficult to play stabilizing role	Increasing proliferation of nuclear and advanced conventional munitions
Creates hegemonic stability	All seek to preserve the overall stability of the system while pursuing national interest	Possibility of Thucydides Trap conflict grows	Increasing number of rogue or failed states
Resists emergence of other hegemons	All seek to exploit secondary conflicts	Conflict increases among 2nd- and 3rd-tier nations	Increasing use of ad hoc transactional diplomacy

How Power Is Distributed within a Hegemonic World

The hegemon unquestionably possesses unchallengeable power across the full spectrum of national resources. It is the world's dominant military power, as measured in terms of the size and diversity of its military resources. It has the biggest army, navy, air force, or whatever else may be the military configuration of the day. It also has the ability to project that power on a regional or global scale. The extensive network of Roman roads, the British fleet, modern-day aircraft carriers, intercontinental missiles and bombers, and rapid deployment forces enable the nations that possess them to extend power beyond their borders. The possession of state-of-the-art military technology also is important, as is the development of new cutting-edge technologies that will dominate any future battlefield.

A hegemon also possesses preponderant economic power, usually giving it the world's largest and most technologically advanced economic capabilities that meet its own economic needs at home and influence other nations through bilateral or multilateral trade arrangements, through the leading role of hegemon-based multinational corporations, and through technological superiority.

Soft power (the ability to influence other nations by example and leadership) also is important to establish the hegemon as the role model to be emulated by other nations. It includes a nation's standing in defining global social and cultural norms, its impact as a role model in terms of domestic politics, economic performance, and international behavior, and its ability to influence other nations through non-coercive means. Also included are other nations' willingness to seek its assistance in international conflict resolution, mediation and peacekeeping, and international social or humanitarian crises.

A hegemon also frequently believes that it possesses a historical manifest destiny to fulfill in the international arena, permitting it to establish a sphere of influence within a particular region; to provide stability in a changing and dangerous world; to defend its domain from hostile external forces; and to propagate its own "superior" religious, cultural, and social norms to "less civilized" peoples. Americans spoke of their "manifest destiny" to expand westward to the Pacific Ocean and then to maintain the Monroe Doctrine, which denied European influence in the New World, thought to be an exclusively American sphere of influence. The French spoke of their "*mission civilisatrice*" to extend their culture and influence to lesser peoples, and the British offered their version of the "White Man's Burden" to similar ends. The Soviet Union thought itself destined to lead the way to the eventual victory of communism on a global scale.

A hegemon frequently seeks to institutionalize its dominance through multilateral organizations and agreements that affirm its disproportional influence and create limited burden sharing by other institutional members. The British-led creation of the Commonwealth of Nations was London's largely symbolic attempt to maintain influence among its former colonies. America's dominant position in the western Cold War alliances, including NATO, also was such an arrangement; while Washington enjoyed de facto first-among-equals status in the alliance, it nonetheless benefited from the contributions of other NATO members. Russian dominance of the Warsaw Treaty Organization and the Council of Mutual Economic Assistance performed a similar function for Moscow.

A hegemon must also possess the political will to lead and effective domestic political institutions through which to do it. A clear sense of direction and commitment and a steady hand at the helm strengthen its leadership. An on-again, off-again commitment to accept the burdens of leadership, or the domestic political instability that results in constantly shifting policies, compromises the hegemon's credibility and weakens the willingness of others to follow its lead.

The dominant role of a hegemon frequently leads to what is called "hegemonic stability," a relatively long period of peace within the international system.[4] The centuries-long dominance of the Roman empire resulted in the *Pax Romana*—the peace of Rome—from 27 BCE to 180 CE, and historians speak of the *Pax Americana* from the end of World War II to the end of the Cold War, the *Pax Britannica* from 1815 to 1914, or the *Pax Sinica* during periods of Chinese dominance in Asia. George

Modelski speaks of a "long cycle" of approximately seventy to one hundred years in which the dominance of a hegemonic power offers peace and stability.[5] He describes five "long cycles," each of which eventually ended with the replacement of the existing hegemon by a new, rising nation-state. These are: (1) the dominant role of Portugal in the sixteenth century; (2) the rise of the Netherlands in the seventeenth century; (3) the rise of Great Britain in the eighteenth century, briefly interrupted by the French revolution and Napoleonic wars; (4) Britain's return to a hegemonic role in the nineteenth century until the outbreak of World War I in 1914; and (5) the rise of the United States as a de facto hegemon during the immediate post–Cold War period.

But even the longest cycles must end. A. F. K. Organski explains such transitions in terms of the impact of rising and declining nations, the former eager to assert their newfound power—Germany and Japan in the late nineteenth and first half of the twentieth centuries—and the latter jealously defensive of their now declining status—Britain or France during the same period and as their empires slipped away after World War II. Either may initiate conflict, although the impatience of a rising power usually results in war more often than the growing desperation of a declining power.[6]

A broader study conducted by Graham Allison finds that among sixteen cases of competition between a declining hegemon and a rising challenger over the last five hundred years, all but four resulted in war.[7] Those four were the rise of Spain over Portugal in the late fifteenth century, the rise of American power to supplant Great Britain at the beginning of the twentieth century, the rise of the Soviet Union to challenge America during the Cold War from 1945 to 1991, and the ascension of Germany as the most powerful nation within the European Union after the Cold War. Three of the four peaceful outcomes resulted from special circumstances: Great Britain purposely chose to accommodate growing American power rather than directly challenge it; the growing power of reunited Germany post-1991 occurred within the context of the European Union and in the face of self-imposed restrictions on

German military power; and the potentially cataclysmic confrontation of the United States and the USSR during the Cold War was mitigated by the fear of mutually assured destruction (MAD), deterrence strategies in both nations, partial arms limitations agreements, and the impact of events such as the Cuban missile crisis. These exceptions aside, fear remains that the general pattern may hold in the future as an ascendant China or an assertive Russia confront American economic and military power, resulting in a so-called Thucydides Trap, named for the Greek historian who described the seemingly inevitable clash between Athens and Sparta, which ultimately weakened both city-states and opened Greece to Persian dominance.

Sources of Stability and Instability

The stability of a well-functioning hegemonic system is enhanced by its relative simplicity and the mutual advantages that flow to the hegemon and the subordinate participants. The absence of disruptive conflict allows for the emergence of extensive trade networks and a sense of common identity and culture. While the hegemon itself occasionally uses military force to deal preemptively with nascent threats and to mediate or outright suppress localized conflict among, or rebellion by, its subordinates, no conflict poses a threat to the stability of the hegemonic system as a whole.

But there are also potential seeds of instability built into the system. The hegemon itself could demand too much of its subordinates, disrupting the balance between perceived benefits and costs to both hegemon and subordinates. The hegemon could become increasingly repressive, crossing the fine line that separates manipulating conflicts from simply imposing one's own will. More broadly, a unipolar system could gradually evolve into a bipolar or limited multipolar system as other nations gain power, or secondary powers could form blocking alliances to thwart the will of the hegemon. More disruptively, a single ascending nation could challenge the hegemon, evoking the Thucydides Trap noted above. Instability also could emerge from changes within the hegemon itself. Lagging economic performance, domestic political instability, and a simple loss of the willingness to continue as a hegemon with all of its costs and responsibilities might lead the hegemon to step back from the role.

If the COVID-19 crisis has taught us anything, it is that the relative stability of any international system must also be measured in terms of its ability to deal with catastrophic challenges. Pandemics are not alone on the list of possible challenges. Joining them are environmental crises, global warming and its impact on weather and sea levels, natural disasters of all sorts, and manmade dislocations like famine or mass migration associated with wars and failed states.

In many ways, a hegemonic system seems particularly well prepared to respond. By definition, the hegemon possesses a disproportionate share of the world economic and military resources. Moreover, it is accustomed to assuming a leadership role, and other nations seem willing to follow its lead. It already plays a leading role in major institutions such as the United Nations, regional blocs, and functional bodies like the World Trade Organization, and has the option of responding to the crises through its multilateral institutional roles or unilaterally, given its exceptional resources.

But capability alone may not be enough. The political will to employ those capabilities must continue to be there. Any powerful nation, and especially a systemic hegemon, may eventually feel itself called upon to contribute more than its fair share; it may suffer from what might be called "crisis fatigue" and a sense that, with the best of intentions, it has overextended itself. In a rapidly changing world characterized by what Fareed Zakaria has described as "the rise of everybody else," even the most generous hegemons periodically may call for an adjustment of the distribution of burdens. At times, such action may apply to a limited range of issues and commitments, or be based on a short-term shift in political power in the hegemon itself; what one administration does, the next can undo. But if the pattern repeats itself in a series of on-again, off-again shifts, or if there is a fundamental and long-term shift in the hegemon's willingness to shoulder the burden of leadership, the hegemonic system will shift toward another pattern, most likely initially a bipolar or limited multipolar system.

What Would a Hegemonic System Look Like in Today's World?

Given the increasing dispersal of economic and military power among a number of nation-states and/or regional blocs, it is unlikely that a global hegemonic system would emerge in today's world. The brief and frequently criticized ascendency of the United States immediately after the end of the Cold War was an aberration, born of uncertainty about the long-term meaning of the disintegration of the Soviet Union. That is not to say, however, that an ascendant nation-state such as China or more powerful nations like the United States or Russia might not aspire to the role.[8] Perception is the key. Any nation-state that other major powers perceived as attempting to establish global hegemony would be met with similar challenges from other ascending nations or de facto blocking alliances among a number of states, friends and foes alike.

More realistic is the possible emergence of what might be called "regional hegemons." Such efforts are now evident in China's attempts to dominate the western Pacific, putting it at odds with neighboring nations like Japan, Vietnam, and India, and intensifying conflict with old enemies like Taiwan. Its extension of economic and military power, coupled with what military analysts call an "area denial strategy" to limit other nations' access to a region, seem designed to create a Chinese sphere of influence. Growing Russian efforts to extend its influence over many of the new independent states that emerged from the breakup of the Soviet Union or the nations of Eastern Europe that had been a part of the Soviet bloc are based on similar motivations. Now capable of playing, at best, a limited global role, Moscow is intensifying its penetration of what Russians call "the near abroad," destabilizing the political and economic life of its neighbors, opposing (with limited success) closer association with the EU and NATO, encouraging de facto American withdrawal from post–World War II institutions, and occasionally directly applying military pressure, as in the seizure of Crimea in 2014 or limited military action against Ukraine.[9]

A NEW BALANCE OF POWER IN A BIPOLAR OR LIMITED MULTIPOLAR WORLD

The next three possible futures—a bipolar or limited multipolar world, a stable multipolar world, and an unstable multipolar world—all have one thing in common: the nature of the international system is determined by a growing number of major powers and by their acceptance of the rules of engagement that spell out their relationship with one another and with less powerful actors. There is a general acceptance that power is not evenly distributed and that those who possess it have a special system-defining role to play. Among themselves, the major powers share a common playbook in periods of relative international stability, setting forth the commonly accepted goals of preventing the rise of a hegemon from among their own number and of promoting stability and relative peace among less powerful nations. In periods of growing instability caused by the ascension of a revisionist state or by conflict among second- and third-tier nations, the international system edges toward anarchy, with the major powers reducing or abandoning their broader responsibilities and focusing on the increasingly fraught relationships among themselves and/or tactically exploiting regional rivalries to their own benefit.

The Structure of a Bipolar or Limited Multipolar World

In the first of these scenarios—a bipolar or limited multipolar world—the international system is configured as either a standoff between two major powers (the early phase of the Cold War from the late-1940s to the mid-1960s) or a more complex arrangement in which the initial bipolar confrontation is altered but not fundamentally changed by the addition of other powerful actors (the Cold War from the mid-1960s to its end, with the breakup of the Soviet Union in 1991, encompassing the rise of the People's Republic of China, the creation of NATO and the European Union, the spread of nuclear weapons, and the growth of a neutralist bloc). In many ways, such systems offer a rare sense of clarity: even at their most complex moments, the fundamental issues are defined either in terms of which "side" you are on or how you position your nation to avoid direct commitment and maintain tactical flexibility.[10]

For the major players, the goals are simple, at least in theory. Stability is maintained by a few major powers balancing their competing interests with the broader need for regional or global stability. A major power must maintain a position of relative strength vis-à-vis the primary adversary. This usually evokes a shifting balance of power, complex alliance systems, and some form of mutual deterrence. At the same time, the key players must craft a playbook for dealing with potentially disruptive secondary conflicts in ways that are mutually accepted by the major players. This usually involves the grudging acceptance of spheres of influence, common agreement on how major powers can step in to mediate or intervene in lesser conflicts, and formal or informal agreement that major powers will exercise some level of mutual restraint to prevent secondary conflicts from turning into major power confrontations. Most often, it works, sometimes it doesn't. The limited nature of the Korean war, the mutual agreement that the Vietnam war would not escalate into a direct nuclear confrontation between Washington and Moscow, and the grudging acceptance that little could be done about the Russian annexation of Crimea are good examples of such restraint, while the Cuban missile crisis and the numerous confrontations over Berlin are examples in which both sides edged dangerously close to war.

There are payoffs, and there are risks. Seen in the broader perspective, such arrangements promote but do not guarantee relative stability within the international system. Everybody gets something, but everybody also pays a cost. The major powers benefit from the overall stability within the system and get to focus on the more critically important issues that deal with other first-tier states. But if any existing nation or newcomer seeks to assert overall dominance and aspire to become a hegemon, the others must respond by realigning the balance of power and the formal and informal alliance structures. The major players also benefit from the implied subordination of second- and third-tier nations, which attempt to maneuver opportunistically within the framework imposed by major-power policies but frequently have little choice but to submit to one-sided economic and military arrangements.

But the major powers also pay a cost in asserting their leadership role. Alliances are a two-way street, costing the major powers in terms of military and economic risks associated with possible alliance-related wars as well as requiring the immediate commitment of additional economic and military resources to maintain the alliance structure and readiness. Maintaining solidarity within the alliance is sometimes difficult. During the Cold War, Washington constantly had to deal with resistance from fellow NATO members, especially France, which briefly de facto withdrew from many alliance activities in the 1960s. Moscow had similar problems within the Warsaw Pact, culminating in constant political and economic pressure and occasionally in military action, as in Hungary in 1956 and Czechoslovakia in 1968. Moreover, mediation and peacekeeping efforts to mitigate second- and third-tier conflicts or to deal with growing R2P expectations exact frequently unpredictable and seemingly unending costs, casualties, and political capital both at home and on the international stage.[11]

How Power Is Distributed in a Bipolar or Limited Multipolar World

Bipolar or limited multipolar systems are built around the formation of complex alliance systems that derive their internal cohesion from the economic and military power of the major powers around which alliances cluster, the strength of the perceived mutual threat or potential benefits, the voluntary or coercive nature of the alliance itself, and a complex assortment of "soft" issues such as a bloc-shared ideology or culture, long-standing historical ties, or a "special relationship." Thus power is distributed *between* competing alliances (NATO and the Warsaw Pact during the Cold War, or the Triple Alliance and the Triple Entente in the run-up to World War I) and *within* alliances (Moscow and the other Warsaw Pact nations, and Washington and other NATO members). Alliance flexibility is frequently a sign of a fundamentally healthy relationship, permitting the association to respond over time to changing issues, waxing and waning external threats, and the volatile nature of domestic politics within the member states.

Strong alliances usually emerge when there is an acknowledged bloc leader, preferably resulting from the consensus of other bloc members rather than coercion by the most powerful nation. During the Cold War, NATO de facto acknowledged American leadership on most issues, although frictions sometimes resulted from both political and technical issues such as the unilateral or shared control of nuclear weapons or the use of American bases for non-NATO-related missions. The Soviet-led Warsaw Treaty Organization was far more tightly centralized, resorting to military intervention to prevent defections in Hungary in 1956 and Czechoslovakia in 1968 and intervening politically in Poland in 1956 and 1981. Only Yugoslavia escaped its grip early in the Cold War in 1948, while Romania carved out limited wiggle room to dissent from bloc policy on issues such as the Middle East.

Weak alliances, on the other hand, undercut bloc ability to speak with a common voice or threaten unified action. Weakness may stem from the absence of a commonly accepted bloc leader; the Triple Entente of Britain, France, and Russia before World War I was hobbled by the long-standing rivalries of its members, while the opposing Triple Alliance of a unified Germany, Austria-Hungary, and Italy was de facto led by Berlin.[12] Also important is the rise of revisionist states external to the alliance. While the rise of China is formally tangential to what survives of the Cold War alliance structures, it nonetheless compels important members to reassess their commitment to an Atlanticist worldview. Disagreement over the common threat level also contributes to disunity, as does discord over the fundamental purpose and identity of the alliance. Both issues now roil NATO, which faces an uncertain future in terms of the American and British commitments, the nature of the threat from Russia, and the rise of populist and anti–European Union regimes.

Also critical to the stability of a bipolar or limited multipolar system is the role of second- and third-tier nations. They are more than just a motley collection of less powerful nations whose interests complicate an otherwise orderly world. From the perspective of the major powers, they are the potential building blocks of larger alliances or less formal associations. They also are the majority of voting members of the United Nations General Assembly, ten of the non-veto-holding votes in the Security Council, and the majority in virtually all of the expanding number of international organizations. They form the core of regional organizations such as the African Union (formerly the Organization of African Unity), the Organization of American States, the Arab League, the Caribbean Community, and others, all of which promote regional cooperation, deal with regional problems, and attempt with mixed success to mediate disputes among member states. Also increasingly important are regional trading blocs such as the European Union, the USMCA, Mercosur (a Latin American trading bloc), the Eurasian Economic Union (a Russian-dominated group of former Soviet states in Central and West Asia), among many others. They are unevenly developed on a global scale, especially in Africa, Latin America, and Southeast Asia, and several nascent blocs may complete among themselves within the same region. Their role is to encourage trade within regions, and they are especially attractive to second- and third-tier nations that may find it difficult to find a niche within larger global trade regimes or to emerging regional hegemons.

Conversely, second- and third-tier nations are also sometimes a source of problems. Political and economic instability are contagious, at first usually to a troubled state's neighbors but eventually to the broader world. Local conflicts have a way of becoming regional or even global issues, especially if they are framed in ways that make them seem a part of the larger confrontations among major powers. Issues like famine, genocide, or human rights violations lead to demands for "somebody" to do "something," pleas that are addressed to the most powerful states or blocs. Sometimes the second- and third-tier issues are inexorably linked to the history of past associations through colonialism or foreign domination, creating demands for preferential treatment, compensation, or the New International Economy Order (NIEO), which focuses on North-South economic issues.

Second- and third-tier states employ a number of strategies to maneuver within a bipolar or limited multipolar world. During the Cold War, a neutralist bloc formed, claiming to be a force for peace between the West and East, and frequently becoming the launching pad for nations like Yugoslavia, India, or Indonesia and their charismatic leaders. In other cases, they would take sides in the regional manifestations of Cold War disputes, seeking political, economic, and, frequently, military support from Washington or Moscow.

Conflict within a bipolar or limited multipolar system is managed in a number of ways. Disputes between the major powers are the most disruptive. Under the best circumstances they are avoided by mutual deterrence or dealt with through direct negotiation between those directly involved, sometimes with the help of mediation by other major powers concerned with preserving the overall stability or neutralist nations hoping to play an important role. During the Cold War, Great Britain often cast itself as a channel of communication between Washington and Moscow, and India occasionally played the same role between Washington and Beijing. Conflicts involving only second- or third-tier client states or alliance partners tend to be dealt with on an ad hoc basis. More potentially disruptive are such conflicts among client states belonging to opposing blocs or alliances, which can threaten to escalate into major power confrontations. The Vietnam War is a good example of the destructiveness of such conflicts and major-power efforts to avoid direct confrontation between themselves. Conflicts within second- or third-tier nations caused by civil wars, the collapse of the local government, or humanitarian issues such as genocide or famine are frequently dealt with by direct intervention, preferably on an ad hoc multilateral basis or through the auspices of the United Nations, the EU, or other bodies.

Causes of Stability and Instability in a Bipolar or Limited Multipolar World

Stability within a bipolar or limited multipolar system is facilitated by a mutually accepted relationship among the major powers, usually institutionalized through military and economic alliances and underpinned by the mutual acceptance of a common playbook. The playbook is understood and accepted, however grudgingly, by all the major players, and the costs and benefits are clearly understood. A sense of mutual restraint is present, enforced by the deterrent nature of the confrontation and a "comfort level" for most players, who have learned how to play the game. Everyone understands the risks and consequences, and no one is willing to convert the relationship into a zero-sum, winner-take-all game. Alliance structures are reasonably stable, despite the occasional effort of some secondary members to test the limits of dissent or defection, and everyone understands—or thinks they understand—the red lines that cannot be crossed.

Instability, on the other hand, results from a number of factors. Revisionist states and ascending nations may challenge the core of the old order, forcing the major powers to oppose them or attempt to integrate them into the existing order as peacefully as possible. All too frequently, the major powers make the politically expedient choice of resisting change and refusing to acknowledge the existence of new realities, making the eventual confrontation all the more violent and disruptive. The growing economic and military power of second- and third-tier nations also challenges the existing hierarchy, especially on a regional basis. India, Pakistan, Brazil, Iran, and Saudi Arabia are all seeking greater recognition as ascending powers. The loss of empire or a well-defined sphere of influence, such as Russian power in Eastern Europe, fundamentally changed the post–Cold War world, as did the subsequent expansion of NATO into the region. Declining national power or political instability within the major states also is significant, as is the potential revival of a sense of isolationism or withdrawal from international arrangements and commitments. Whatever the formal outcome of Brexit, Britain will never quite be the same, and its ability to punch above its weight will further deteriorate.

Bipolar and limited multipolar systems should also be relatively well positioned to deal with catastrophic shocks to the system like pandemics, natural disasters, or social upheavals. Collectively the economic, political, and institutional resources are present, especially among the top-tier nations, and there is a reasonably stable pattern of interaction guided by a mutually accepted playbook that has facilitated a high level of cooperation in the past. Effective action would likely depend upon a shared perception of the nature of the threat and its relative impact on the major players. But if the crisis is seen as a wedge issue that reshapes past formal and informal alignments, or if the sense of "we're in this together" shifts to "we win and you lose" or vice versa, past patterns of cooperation would mean little. The best that could be hoped for would be that new ad hoc patterns of cooperation emerged, possibly to be institutionalized if the problem persists, or that dissenting nations opted out of the existing arrangements on this one issue alone but continued their engagement on other important issues, preserving a diminished but still operational version of the old order.

What Would It Be Like If a Bipolar or Limited Multipolar World Emerged Today (or, More Correctly, Reemerged)?

It many ways, we've already seen this reemergence in the Cold War from 1945 to 1991. From 1945 to the mid-1960s, the Cold War alignment was essentially bipolar, with Washington and Moscow putting into place the major political, military, and economic institutions that defined virtually all aspects of the confrontation. From the mid-1960s onward, the system shifted toward a limited multipolar configuration. While the formal institutions remained in place, they now functioned within a more complex and pluralistic world. Washington and Moscow now found it was difficult to deal with alliance partners. A host of newly independent nations emerged, changing international institutions and creating a neutralist bloc. Fundamental economic changes created an emerging global economy. And through it all, the international system survived and adapted, but not without conflict and disruption, especially in local and regional wars, but nonetheless without global nuclear war. Not a perfect scorecard, but an acceptable one in light of how things might have played out.

That said, could we go back to such a system at some point in the future? Yes, but probably not quite in the same form. Competition among the major powers—the United States, China, and Russia—would remain a continuing feature of any bipolar or limited multipolar system, and the possible configurations and alignments are complex. Would each create its own alliance system, complete with military and economic arrangements? Would two form an alliance of convenience against the third (Russia and China against the United States seems the most obvious short-term tactical arrangement)? Where will the EU fit in? How would fundamental changes among the second- or third-tier nations change the dynamics of major power interaction in a world characterized by greater pluralism and "the rise of everybody else"?[13] What we do know is that the international system has already been down that road and learned how to survive its dangers and complexities.

A STABLE MULTIPOLAR WORLD

The Structure of a Stable Multipolar World

The major difference between a bipolar or limited multipolar world and a stable multipolar world lies in the growing complexity and pluralism of the international community. The number of major or near-major powers increases; no longer limited to a handful of powerful nations tracing their status back to the nineteenth century or the Cold War, they now comprise a growing list of older and newly empowered nation-states that claim their preeminence because of the collapse of colonial empires, the policies of authoritarian modernizers who rapidly transformed their nations, the impact of globalization, and the proliferation of nuclear and conventional weapons. The Group of Seven (G-7), a once-exclusive association of otherwise diverse economic powers initially created in 1973, is now joined on the international stage by the Group of Twenty (G-20), an expanded version that includes an even more diverse assortment of new global and/or regional powers. No one doubts that its membership will expand in the future. While the initial members continue to possess great resources in absolute terms, the rise of other nations has diminished their relative standing in terms of global impact, resulting in what Fareed Zakaria calls "the rise of everybody else." A new category of rising nations has expanded our descriptive vocabulary. "Ascending powers" or "emerging market economies" now occupy a middle ground amid the traditional "first world" (the major Western economic and military powers, especially during the Cold War), "second world" (a term that has not been used since the end of the Cold War for major communist nations like the USSR or China and their allies), and "third" or "fourth" worlds (all of the other lesser economic and military powers, once seemingly relegated to the motley and disunited category of "underdeveloped countries" and "small powers"). While the membership of the "7s" and the "20s" will be discussed below, suffice it to say that their proliferation, diversity, and growing economic, military, political, and diplomatic roles have revised the structure of the international system and the rules by which it operates.

Equally important is the changing nature of all of the rest of the nation-states that make up the international system. First the staggering numbers: when the United Nations was created just after World War II, it had 51 members; it now has 193.[14] Just about everything changed as that number grew. Vast colonial empires disintegrated, as did major states such as the Soviet Union and Yugoslavia; globalization spread economic power and linked the world in a web of international supply chains and consumerism; military capabilities quickly proliferated as both nuclear and advanced conventional weapons came within the reach of more nations; and for better or worse, a global culture emerged, initially dominated by the West and then growing more diverse as others made their contribution.

That said, the increasing size and diversity of the international community also has created problems. Once dominated by Cold War or essentially major-power concerns, the international community now has to deal with the conflicts and disputes of all of the new players. Local or regional conflicts take center stage, no longer primarily defined by their

Cold War implications and dealt with in a way that avoided escalation into major-power confrontations.

A stable multipolar world also possesses less of what we have termed a common "playbook" from which to operate. Whatever its geographic or cultural biases and shortcomings, the common playbook of the nineteenth-century balance of power and the Cold War shared some common themes about how to play the game. Rooted in a common and almost exclusively European and Atlanticist perspective, and in several centuries of common though conflicted history, it set forth certain expectations. Major powers were expected to manage their mutual animosities and ambitions through diplomacy, and would-be revisionist nations or hegemons were to be controlled by flexible alliances or gradually co-opted into the system by concessions. Disputes among second- or third-tier nations were to be managed in ways that did not disrupt the system as a whole. It was a major power and largely Atlanticist perspective, and dismissive of and unfair to others, but it did provide guidelines for the major players of the day. To be sure, the playbook could not prevent the outbreak of war in 1914 and 1939, when the rise of revisionist nations or the failure of the balance-of-power system or the League of Nations opened the door for the fundamental revision of the international system.

With the proliferation and growing diversity of new players, the playbook became more complex after World War II. It reflected a far broader spectrum of histories and cultures, it raised new and different goals and expectations for new nation-states and the international community as a whole, and it gave voice to old and new lines of division and conflict. While there was a sense that a new and more universal and global playbook would eventually emerge, it was slow to come, especially in telling a more complex world how to translate broad platitudes into a new international order. A work still in progress, the post–Cold War playbook must now attempt to bridge the gaps between the diversities of these cultures and expectations.

How Power Is Distributed in a Stable Multipolar World

Despite the greater complexity, there are still some identifiable criteria that define the pecking order. First-tier powers possess significant assets across the entire spectrum by which power is measured: economic power (measured in terms of massive gross domestic product [GDP], involvement in extensive global and regional trade, and advanced technology); military power (measured in terms of large armed forces, advanced military technology, and the ability to project that power on a regional or global basis); "soft" power (measured in terms of the nation's ability to win the respect of other nations through its stature as a role model and respected member of the international community); and diplomacy (measured in terms of a nation's role as key player in bilateral diplomacy, a leader within international bodies, or a mediator of disputes involving other nations). That said, all first-tier nations are not equal. Some, like the United States, have been at the top of the list since World War II but are now challenged by the rise of other nations, like China, and a resurgent Russia or by the globalization of economic and military resources. Others, like Great Britain or France, still make the cut into the great-powers club, sustained by diminished but still significant economic and military capabilities and the inertia from their once preeminent status. Germany and Japan are unique cases: powerful and disruptive revisionist states in the first half of the twentieth century, they emerged as economic but not military powers after World War II and are now considering further rearmament and a normalization of their international role. Russia also is a unique case: a major superpower during the Cold War, second only to the United States, it declined rapidly after the fall of communism and the breakup of the Soviet Union, only to claw its way back to major-power status under the leadership of Vladimir Putin. China is the wild card. Once a second-tier nation even within the communist bloc, it has risen to the status of a major global power in every sense of the term, intent on demonstrating its newfound power and demanding acceptance of its ascendant role in the international community.

Table 2.2 sets forth several different efforts to establish the international hierarchy of major or near-major powers. It includes the *U.S. News and World Report* "Power Ranking," an overall assessment of a nation's power based on its leadership, economic and military influence, involvement with international alliances, and military strength;[15] the "The Top 20 Economies in the World" assessment by Investopedia, focusing on economic power;[16] the Global Firepower ranking of military power, which generates the composite "Power Index" (in which the lower the index score, the more powerful the nation);[17] and the "Soft Power" ranking by the USC Center for Public Diplomacy.[18] Two caveats are in order. First, the rankings are not directly comparable, although they are a rough guide to where a nation fits into the pecking order. Second, while there is remarkable consistency at the top of the list, there is considerable disagreement about the ranking of the second- or third-tier powers.

Table 2.2. Power Rankings

US *News* Power Ranking	Top Twenty Economies (GDP, in billions [B] or trillions [T] of dollars)	Global Firepower Composite Index	Soft Power
1. United States	1. United States (21.4 T)	1. United States (.0606)	1. France
2. Russia	2. China (14.1 T)	2. Russia (.0681)	2. United Kingdom
3. China	3. Japan (5.2 T)	3. China (.0691)	3. Germany
4. Germany	4. Germany (3.9 T)	4. India (.0953)	4. Sweden
5. United Kingdom	5. India (2.9 T)	5. Japan (.1501)	5. United States
6. France	6. United Kingdom (2.7 T)	6. South Korea (.1509)	6. Switzerland

Table 2.2 (cont.)

US News Power Ranking	Top Twenty Economies (GDP, in billions [B] or trillions [T] of dollars)	Global Firepower Composite Index	Soft Power
7. Japan	7. France (2.6 T)	7. France (.1702)	7. Canada
8. Israel	8. Italy (2.0 T)	8. United Kingdom (.1717)	8. Japan
9. South Korea	9. Brazil (1.9 T)	9. Egypt (.1872)	9. Australia
10. Saudi Arabia	10. Canada (1.7 T)	10. Brazil (.1988)	10. Netherlands
11. United Arab Emirates	11. Russia (1.6 T)	11. Turkey (.2098)	11. Italy
12. Canada	12. South Korea (1.6 T)	12. Italy (.2111)	12. Norway
13. Switzerland	13. Spain (1.4 T)	13. Germany (.2186)	13. Spain
14. India	14. Australia (1.4 T)	14. Iran (.2191)	14. Denmark
15. Australia	15. Mexico (1.3 T)	15. Pakistan (.2364)	15. Finland
16. Turkey	16. Indonesia (1.1 T)	16. Indonesia (.2544)	. . .
17. Italy	17. Netherlands (849 B)	17. Saudi Arabia (.3034)	27. China
18. Qatar	18. Saudi Arabia (779 B)	18. Israel (.3111)	30. Russia
19. Spain	19. Turkey (744 B)	19. Australia (.3225)	
20. Sweden	20. Switzerland (715 B)	20. Spain (.3388)	

The *U.S. News and World Report* ranking places the United States, Russia, and China at the top, with Germany, Great Britain, France, Japan, Israel, South Korea, and Saudi Arabia completing the top ten. The "Top Twenty Economies" lists the top three as the United States, China, and Japan, with Germany, India, Great Britain, France, Italy, Brazil, and Canada next in line; Russia falls to eleventh place in terms of economic standing. "Global Firepower" names the United States, Russia, and China in the top three, with India, Japan, South Korea, France, Great Britain, Egypt, Brazil, Turkey, Italy, and Germany next in line. The "Soft Power" assessment differs substantially. France, Great Britain, Germany, and Sweden lead the list, with the United States dropping to fifth place in 2019, down from its first-place ranking in 2016. Switzerland, Canada, Japan, Australia, and the Netherlands finish out the top ten. China is a distant twenty-seventh, with Russia just behind at thirtieth. Among the acknowledged nuclear powers are the United States, Russia, Great Britain, France, China, India, Pakistan, and North Korea. Israel also is an unacknowledged member of the nuclear club. Iran is on the brink of acquiring nuclear capabilities, and others such as Saudi Arabia are considering their acquisition. South Africa, Ukraine, Belarus, and Kazakhstan have given up nuclear weapons, the first as a consequence of the end of apartheid and the latter three with the end of the Cold War. Libya similarly ended its nuclear weapons development program.

At the top there is remarkable consistency. As noted, the United States can claim bragging rights because it is still at the head of the pack, with the exception of soft power; it is too early to tell whether the drop from first to fifth place is a short-term reaction to the election of a president deeply unpopular with most of the world, or the beginning of a long-term downward spiral. Russia and China also have much to celebrate, except in "Soft Power." Beijing's growing status as a global power is the result of a long-term development strategy reaching back to the era of Deng Xiaoping's economic reforms in the 1980s and Xi Jinping's more recent assertion of Chinese national interests. Russia's reemergence as a regional and perhaps a global power is linked to the economic recovery after the breakup of the Soviet Union and to the strong and increasingly authoritarian leadership of Vladimir Putin.

There is much less consistency just below the top three or four power-ful nations. New rapidly advancing nations appear, confirming the spread of global economic and military power and adding a growing number of non-European nations and former colonies to the list. The *U.S. News and World Report*'s power ranking adds Germany (ranked fourth), Great Brit-ain (fifth), and France (sixth). Below this point, the list grows increasingly diverse, including Japan (seventh), Israel (eighth), South Korea (ninth), and Saudi Arabia (tenth). The next ten are even more eclectic, including, from eleven to twenty, the United Arab Emirates, Canada, Switzerland, India, Australia, Turkey, Italy, Qatar, Spain, and Sweden.

Rankings based on economic power show a similar pattern. The United States, China, and Japan lead the list. Completing the top ten adds a variety of European and emerging economic powers. Germany is fourth, followed by India (fifth), Great Britain (sixth), France (seventh), Italy (eighth), Brazil (ninth), and Canada (tenth). The next ten are more diverse: in rank order they are Russia, South Korea, Spain, Australia, Mex-ico, Indonesia, the Netherlands, Saudi Arabia, Turkey, and Switzerland.

Military power rankings are even more diversified. The United States, Russia, and China lead the list once again, followed by India, Japan, South Korea, France, Great Britain, Egypt, and Brazil, to complete the top ten. The next ten include Turkey, Italy, Germany, Iran, Pakistan, Indonesia, Saudi Arabia, Israel, Australia, and Spain. Adding nuclear weapons to the equation confirms the continuing post–Cold War dominance of the United States and Russia. Russia currently leads with 6,800 warheads, with the United States just behind, at 6,600. In contrast, other nuclear powers' arsenals are small, with France at 300, China at 270, Great Britain at 215, Pakistan at 140, India at 130, Israel at 80, and North Korea at an estimated 20.[19]

As noted, soft power presents an entirely different hierarchy. From its former top ranking in 2016, the United States has slipped to fifth place; the top three are France, Great Britain, and Germany. The other members of the top ten include Sweden (fourth), Switzerland (sixth), Canada (seventh), Japan (eighth), Australia (ninth), and the Netherlands (tenth). China ranks twenty-seventh, with Russia two steps lower at thirtieth.

Another way to assess the first-tier nations in a stable multipolar system is to look at the Group of Seven (G-7) and Group of Twenty (G-20) membership.[20] Both list the most powerful nations in terms of economic status. The G-7 emerged informally in 1973 and included a smaller core of four nations that met after the global oil crisis. This produced a commitment of their finance ministers to meet periodically to deal with similar economic shocks. The group gradually expanded to include its present seven members: the United States, Great Britain, Canada, France, Germany, Italy, and Japan, whose economies represent just under 50 percent of the world's gross domestic product. The European Union also holds a seat, as did post-communist Russia from 1998 to 2014, when it was expelled following the Russian annexation of Crimea. Over time, the G-7's agenda expanded to include a broader assortment of issues, including the management of the international monetary system, assistance to emerging economies, economic stabilization, and related topics such as the environment and global warming. Two sorts of meetings occur, the first involving finance ministers (usually twice a year) and the second bringing together heads of governments (annually), at which informal meetings of world leaders on the sidelines sometimes deal with important international issues beyond the formal G-7 agenda.

Over time, the G-7 experience led to calls for a broader and more diverse assembly, now called the G-20. Formally created in 1999, it included the original G-7 core (including the EU), plus Argentina, Brazil, China, India, Indonesia, Mexico, Russia, Saudi Arabia, South Africa, South Korea, and Turkey. Together, G-20 members account for 90 percent of world GDP and 80 percent of world trade. In 2009 the G-20 was designated as the primary economic forum of wealthy nations, although the G-7 continues to function. Like the smaller body, the G-20's agenda has expanded to include a broader spectrum of international as well as economic issues, and pressure is growing to expand membership to include more nations.

The G-20 more clearly demonstrates the increasing diversity of the nations at the top of the international pecking order. Geographically, they span the globe, with six from Europe (including the separate seat for the European Union), four from Asia, three from North America, two each from South America, South Asia, and the Middle East, and one from Africa. Ten are former colonies, including the United States, Argentina, Australia, Brazil, Canada, India, Indonesia, Mexico, South Africa, and South Korea. Eight are former colonial powers, including those that established overseas empires (Great Britain, France, Germany, Italy, Japan, and the United States) and those that absorbed adjacent territory into their empires (Russia/Soviet Union and Ottoman Turkey). Most of the former colonies probably enjoy the irony that they now sit as de jure equals to their colonial masters in the G-20. Four (Argentina, Mexico, Brazil, and Indonesia) probably enjoy the even greater irony that their former masters aren't at the table at all.

The even more diverse assortment of nations commonly listed as the "next-in-line" or "emerging" powers continues the trend toward greater diversity. While there is no complete agreement on who should be on the list or the precise pecking order, a number of countries usually make the cut, including Colombia, Iran, Israel, Nigeria, Pakistan, Poland, Chile, Israel, Malaysia, Vietnam, the Netherlands, Norway, Greece, Spain, Taiwan, Sweden, the Philippines, and Qatar.

Not surprisingly, the top-tier nations in a stable multipolar world exercise their power in many different ways. The big three—the United States, China, and Russia—have a wide range of choices because of their considerable and diversified resources. Unilateral action is always possible, and perhaps increasingly likely in a world in which multilateral institutions are under increasing challenges. The American invasion of Iraq and the Russian annexation of Crimea are a few of many examples. Although China primarily exploits its economic power—the Belt and Road Project to extend its economic and diplomatic influence by drawing its partners into a Chinese-controlled global trading network, for example—its expanding military power and assertiveness on the world stage increase its leverage.

First-tier nations also may exploit their influence within international or regional bodies. The five permanent members of the UN Security Council still hold a veto over its actions, although they sometimes build majority support in both the Security Council and General Assembly over issues that do not involve the direct interest of the veto-holding members. Major-power action through regional bodies is also possible; NATO-based intervention in the conflicts that grew out of the breakup of Yugoslavia in the early 1990s and Organization of American States–approved sanctions against an increasingly repressive regime in Venezuela in 2018 are but two examples. Major-power led "coalitions of the willing"—ad hoc alliances such as the American intervention in Iraq to deal with nonexistent "weapons of mass destruction"—provide the cover for major-power action accompanied by largely token assistance from other countries either traditionally regarded as loyal allies or wishing to curry favor with the coalition leader.

Independent action by less powerful nations is more difficult. Even those close to the top, such as Great Britain, France, Germany, or Japan, still have far more limited resources at their disposal. Exploiting special relationships, employing multilateral approaches through global or regional bodies, and building ad hoc coalitions on specific issues are better tactical choices. Even then, the growing number of first- and second-tier nations, evidenced by the G-7 and more recently the G-20, makes the task increasingly difficult. Those even lower on the pecking order below the G-20 face even greater problems. While unilateral action on issues of great importance to such nations may be accepted, or perhaps merely tolerated, their freedom of action is restricted on issues of interest to the broader international community. For them, broad multilateral action and coalition building on specific issues such as global economic development, North-South economic ties, migration, or human rights are better tactical choices.

Sources of Stability and Instability in a Stable Multipolar World

The sources of stability in a multipolar world are rooted in a widespread acceptance of the different roles that various nation-states play and in an acceptance of the playbook that shapes their interaction. Not surprisingly in such a complex world, there are many different roles to be acted out on many different stages. Change is constant. Individual nation-states move up and down the pecking order and in and out of different situations and relationships that require nuanced responses. Some nation-states will always seem to be at or near the top, others will be much further down, and most will be somewhere in the middle, aspiring to a greater role but understanding the realities of global power and position. Stability depends on managing all of these roles in ways that create and sustain a workable international system. "Workable" does not always mean peaceful, at least in the literal sense. Conflict is inevitable, and in a world in which power is measured in economic, military, and "soft" terms, it will take many overlapping forms. "Workable" simply means that the system manages to process and channel these conflicts in ways that leave the overall system functioning in a sustainable fashion.

Critical to this sense of balance are the roles that will be played by the major powers at the top of the pecking order. They come to their roles with considerable historical baggage from two world wars, the Cold War, the loss of empires, and the heritage of two socialist revolutions in Russia and China. While shaped by those events, they must realize that a stable multipolar world in the twenty-first century requires a new perspective. Most importantly, they must now manage their roles and responsibilities with new realities in mind. Long-term stability will depend on this on many fronts. The United States will have to deal with being a lesser first among equals as its relative power declines, and perhaps with growing domestic pressure to step back from its once welcomed leadership role. Great Britain and France will have to continue to cope with declining military and economic power and with the implications of their relationship with the European Union (Britain out with the Brexit decision, and France facing changes within the EU from German reunification and the eastward expansion of the EU and NATO). Germany and Japan will face the need to sustain their postwar economic success along with the need to play a greater diplomatic and military role on the world stage. Russia and China seem intent on playing the role of ascending and revisionist powers, potentially disruptive postures that challenge the other top-tier nations to peacefully manage or successfully contain these rising powers or prepare for an eventual confrontation.

The second-tier powers now expanding the ranks of the G-20 or aspiring to upward economic and military mobility also have a critical role to play in sustaining an adaptive multipolar system. In many ways, they are both the success stories of the post–World War II world and the role models for other nations lower on the pecking order. How they play their roles will be important to the transformation of the system toward even greater multipolarity. Balance will be needed. Aggressive challenges to the remaining, although diminished, great powers will undercut their role in managing the transition and containing conflict, while timidity and excessive caution will slow the overall movement toward an increasingly stable and self-sustaining multipolar world.

Domestic political stability within the top-tier nations is also key to the effective operation of a stable multipolar system. That does not mean that change will not occur; governments will come and go, as they always have. But there will be a threshold, easy to describe but hard to find, beyond which the normal ebb and flow of political change fundamentally alters the overall international system itself. Newly assertive revisionist nations can tip the balance, as can a nation's willingness to abandon a once prominent role and hand off responsibility to others. The rise of China and the return of Russia, as well as the growing assertiveness of Turkey, India, and Iran at the regional level, are good examples of the first pattern, while the U.S. shift away from multilateral institutions and Britain's withdrawal from the EU illustrate the second. New issues and new or reanimated national identities or ideologies will have their impact on the domestic politics of many nations, and how they deal with them will in turn shape the international system. Global warming, human rights, income inequalities within and among nations, and the emergence of populist and nationalist movements are but a few of a growing list of topics that will in some way challenge the international order.

Economic stability is also important, both within the leading national economies and in the broader global economy. As with politics, change is inevitable. Nations will move up and down the economic pecking order in response to their own developmental and trading strategies, and the normal ups and downs of business cycles will take their toll. Fundamental shocks to the economic system could have a major destabilizing impact. An economic crisis like that of 2008, the euro and sovereign debt crises from 2009 to 2010, or concern about a sustained downturn in the global economy as a whole will impact a nation's commitment to institutions like the World Trade Organization, the World Bank, and the International Monetary Fund, as well as regional trading blocs and institutions like the EU and the European Stability Mechanism crafted since the Bretton Woods Conference.

Also important to the long-term stability of a multipolar system will be its ability to deal with local and regional conflicts. A multipolar world is a natural breeding ground for such conflicts. With no overarching hegemon or balance of power in place, and no fundamental division of the world into competing bipolar blocs as in the Cold War, nations will be able to indulge in long-standing conflicts over borders, cultural and religious differences, or whatever has divided them in the past. The first-tier nations and those newly ascendant to the G-20 will have to play a proactive role to mitigate such conflicts, but there will also be the temptation to meddle in them for their own purposes. "Failed states," themselves frequently the product of unresolved local conflicts, will add to the burden of local and regional peacekeeping. The endless occurrence of natural disasters, famines, and forced migrations that require humanitarian intervention will also place great burdens on the political will and resources of nations that have accepted to the R2P mandate.

Important to the stability of a multipolar system will be its ability to respond to catastrophic challenges like pandemics, natural disasters, and other shocks to the system. The economic, social, and institutional resources will all be there, as evidenced by the system's overall ability to mobilize them to bear on more conventional issues of war and peace. But new challenges will present new opportunities for both success and failure. By definition, the greater number and diversity of players will complicate the game, as will the greater complexity of the formal and informal institutional arrangements. There probably will be less of a shared perception of new wedge issues and, therefore, a greater propensity to explore the implications of standing aside from a common effort in the hope of securing gain for individual nations. The role of leadership will be critically important; both the traditional firsts among equals and the ascending nations will have to broadly agree on most, if not all, of the elements of a response to problems that increasingly transcend regional, economic, cultural, and social differences. Political stability within those nations will be important as well, especially to the extent that it shapes their willingness to engage the international system in ways appropriate to their capabilities.

What Would a Stable Multipolar System Look Like in Today's World?

What would a stable multipolar system look like in today's world? In many ways, it's already here. The post–Cold War world possesses most, if not all, of its characteristics: the number of first- or near first-tier nations, evidenced in the membership of the G-7; an emerging assortment of rapidly rising second-tier nations, as demonstrated by the G-20 membership; a growing proliferation of economic, military, and human resources to an increasingly diverse assortment nations from all continents; an expanding number of second- and third-tier nations seemingly committed to membership in a global community and to pursuing a similar path toward further economic and social development; a commitment on the part of first- and second-tier nations to accept at least some of the responsibilities associated with increasing global status; and an extensive, if less than perfect, attempt to institutionalize and codify these responsibilities and understandings into a rule-based system accompanied by a widely shared playbook of how the system is supposed to work. What is not present also is important: there are no fundamental ideological or cultural issues that polarize the world into the us-versus-them divisions of the Cold War; there have been no fundamental military clashes between first-tier nations, although the tensions are rising; there are no fundamentally opposing alliance structures or spheres of influence to divide the world; and, as yet, there have been no regional or local conflicts that have drawn the major powers into direct confrontation.

AN UNSTABLE MULTIPOLAR WORLD

What Would an Unstable Multipolar System Look Like?
Given the complexity of a stable multipolar system, it is worth exploring what the international system would be like in the event of its deterioration into a less stable alternative. As the previous section noted, the checklist of things needed for stability is long and demanding; nations must be internally stable, each must understand and be willing to accept its place in the hierarchy and to play the role implicitly assigned to it, and potentially disruptive secondary conflicts must be kept within acceptable parameters. Easy to say, but difficult to do. That said, there do seem to be some obvious areas in which problems might arise.

First, the major powers—the United States, China, and Russia—might recreate the superpower rivalries of the Cold War. America's relative decline has stoked efforts to reassert its military and economic power and to rethink its commitments to global engagement. China and Russia make no secret of their revisionist goals. The road ahead for all three is littered with possible Thucydides Traps, which, as history tells us, make it highly likely but not certain that ascending and descending nations will provoke major wars. NATO, an important component of the old Cold War confrontation, is still there and perceived by Moscow as a growing threat, and the extensive although troubled economic integration of the West has added to the sense of confrontation. China and the United States spar over influence in the western Pacific and arm for potential conflict. With three players in the game, the possible alignments and strategies are even more complex. While it is far less likely that the rest of the world would split into two or three camps in support of the major players, any sustained confrontation would end the special role of top-tier nations in making a multipolar system viable.

Second, local or regional conflicts could escalate to a level where they challenge the stability of the system. Examples abound. The on-again, off-again wars in the Middle East have always been a source of instability and are now potentially even more disruptive with the assertiveness of Iran and Saudi Arabia and the diminishing likelihood that the Palestinian issue will be solved at the bargaining table. The confrontation between India and Pakistan remains a potential nuclear conflagration. Territorial issues could animate conflicts, most among secondary powers but some involving the major powers themselves, as with the Russian annexation of Crimea or Chinese claims to ultimately take control of Taiwan. Local or regional conflicts also always tempt the major powers to take sides, sometimes in hope of extending their influence into new areas and sometimes merely to flaunt their presence as a global power. Terrorism will remain a source of instability, capable of destabilizing nations and provoking foreign intervention.

Third, growing political and economic instability within nations ultimately will compromise the stability of the international system within which they exist. Such instability may be linked to economic or cultural conflicts, to increasingly dysfunctional institutions, or to growing public dissatisfaction with the "establishment" or the "one percent" or "global elites." A revitalization of national culture and identity or a sense of exceptionalism or manifest destiny can add to the level of conflict, especially if they are linked to efforts to extirpate foreign influence and curb immigration. As a nation turns inward for a sense of renewed identity and purpose, it also turns a more isolationist and hostile face to the outside world.

As a worst-case scenario, the deterioration of a stable multipolar system and the individual nation-states that once played key roles in its operation could lead to the creation of a world of disorder. It wouldn't be pretty. The increasing dysfunction of once-viable nation-states would undercut the stability of the international system. Growing disorder within the broader system as a whole would compromise its ability to cope with international challenges and weaken the nation-states' willingness to turn to it for solutions. Each problem exacerbates the other. A downward spiral of decreasing capabilities and commitments would result to a race to the bottom. Top-tier nations that once led the multipolar system might no longer have the capability or the will to play that role. Second- and third-tier nations that once understood or perhaps just grudgingly accepted the realities of a multipolar would lose a clear sense of their place and role within the system, perhaps either liberating them to play a more assertive leadership role or tempting them to disruptively assert their own demands. Commitments to global, regional, or multilateral institutions or treaties would weaken as nations increasingly resorted to direct bilateral arrangements, transactional and ad hoc diplomacy, and self-help measures to protect themselves in an every-nation-for-itself world. The major powers would become even more protective of their national interests, perhaps recreating a bi- or tripolar world restrained only by mutual deterrence. The second- and third-tier nations would opportunistically pursue their own interests, with little commitment to a common set of global institutions or a playbook.

Before we begin to examine the potential decline and fall of a stable multipolar system, we should have a clear understanding of what "dysfunctional" means. It doesn't necessarily mean that the world has fallen into the abyss. There will still be a "system" of sorts, and nation-states will still exist as the primary players. In many ways, the nation-states will become even more important as they reassert their sovereignty and distinctive national interests, now operating within an increasingly leaderless and de-institutionalized world. Defining "dysfunction" will be a judgment call on the part of the analyst, not an absolute and measurable outcome. For our purposes, which are to describe and analyze different possible international systems, dysfunction is simply the system's inability to do whatever it was created to do. Easy to say, difficult to measure. International systems do not spontaneously emerge; they usually are the product of some conscious design on the part of nations trying to cope with whatever ended the previous order of things. The winners come together to plan a new set of arrangements to bring order or at least to not make the same mistakes again. Sometimes they succeed for a relatively long period of time, as with the Treaty of Westphalia, balance of power, and post–World War II arrangements, complicated but not destroyed by the Cold War. Sometimes they fail, as with the League of Nations. And sometimes the outcome is uncertain, as with today's post–Cold War world now rethinking its commitment to globalization and multilateralism.

What does that mean in the real world? In terms of a stable multilateral system, it means several things. First, can the system contain and channel potential conflicts among the major powers? Can it deal with ascendant powers, especially among what we have described as the bottom half of the G-20 and those even further down the pecking order? Can it cope with new social, economic, and humanitarian issues that clamor for attention? Can it manage rogue and failed states? Success does not mean a perfect scorecard, and some things are more important than others. In the short term, avoiding major-power conflicts is at the top of the list, with the caveat that lesser conflicts have a way of growing into major confrontations if left unattended. Long-term systemic stability also means managing the ascent and decent of the "wannabes" and the "used-to-bes." Maintaining a widely accepted playbook of informal and institutionalized rules and modus operandi is also important. At least minimally coping with some of the social, economic, and humanitarian issues is somewhere further down the list of success criteria, clouded by the reality that political considerations frequently dictate such commitments. For all nations, there must be a reason to accept a system as useful, if not perfect. The game must be worth the candle.

What does "dysfunctional" mean in our assessment of the nation-states that operate within the system? Again, it's a judgment call. But there is little doubt that prolonged political instability, institutional gridlock, debilitating partisanship, and increasing public denial of the legitimacy of the existing order severely compromise any government's ability to play a constructive role on the international stage. "Performance legitimacy" is also important; it refers to any government's ability to meet the day-to-day needs of its people, from maintaining public order and keeping the government and the economy open for business as usual to collecting garbage and plowing the streets in winter. Economic failure, widening income inequality, and growing social polarization along ethnic, ideological, or class lines also take their toll. It is tempting and frequently politically expedient to shift the blame for all of these maladies to external causes. Jobs were outsourced to low-labor-cost nations; the market was flooded by imported products; immigrants changed the domestic labor market and perhaps the nation's culture and politics as well; rural areas and small towns were hollowed out as the increasingly sophisticated and globalized cities grew to new dominance; and the traditional culture was rejected or just forgotten in the face of the global reach of "McWorld." The problem is not "us," but "them" and the international system within which they operate. Understandably, if nonetheless disruptively, nations in internal crises are tempted to turn inward to heal themselves before, if ever, returning to an important role in the international community.

The Structure of an Unstable Multipolar World

The earlier sense of order and place that defined where a nation fit into the pecking order and the role assigned to it is now open to reinterpretation. The sense of hierarchy is now uncertain. The definition of first- and second-tier nations becomes less clear, and the hierarchy is disputed by ascending and descending powers. Potential conflict among the first-tier nations—the United States, Russia, and China, in this case—becomes increasingly more likely and potentially disruptive. Preoccupied by these prospects, the major powers are less willing or able to play their once vital stabilizing role, increasingly seeing all issues on the global agenda through the lens of their own particular fears and aspirations. The maintenance of a viable overall international system, dealing with rogue and failed states, regional conflicts, and the endless responsibilities that come with being a major power become less important as they turn their attention and resources to the sharpening confrontation among themselves. Once-stable alliances and multilateral arrangements now seem less able to provide security or to meet the demands of ascending powers and revisionist powers, leading them to abandon or redefine such relationships and turn to unilateral and self-help solutions.

Change at the top of the pecking order has broad implications for all of the other elements of the system. Existing international bodies like the UN will face growing demands and declining resources as they attempt to fill in the void caused by diminished leadership from the major powers. In some cases, they will succeed, especially if second-tier nations step up to provide new leadership in key areas such as peacekeeping and crisis management and if the veto-holding members of the Security Council stand aside, except when their interests are directly challenged. In other broader areas such as social and human services, human rights, and other R2P issues, major powers' track records will be far less impressive, further eroding confidence in their viability to act in a rapidly changing world.

Regional multilateral economic and military institutions also will be challenged. Growing confrontation among the major powers will force a redefinition of regional defense arrangements. The us-or-them clarity of the Cold War will be replaced by a more confusing set of choices for most nations. Ad hoc alliances will become more commonplace, hopefully meeting short-term economic or national security needs but lacking the clarity of long-term commitments. With once seemingly certain arrangements such as the EU, NATO, and the WTO now open to question, it will be a new world of both danger and opportunity.

In a less certain and structured multilateral world, regional or local conflicts will become potentially far more destructive. The growing confrontations between Saudi Arabia and Iran, increasingly linked to American and Russian involvement, will further destabilize an already volatile region, as will the likely failure to deal with the Palestinian question in a way acceptable to all sides. India and Pakistan will continue on the brink of a regional nuclear war. The expansion of Chinese influence and military presence in the western Pacific will create ever more potential flashpoints. Increasing ethnic, religious, and cultural conflicts will spread throughout South Asia and Africa.

Economic crises also will take their toll. Great Britain's withdrawal from the EU will severely impact both the British and European economies, at least in the short run. The potential departure of other nations intent on reasserting their own sovereignty and national identity will loom in the background, as will the potential failure of the euro, the common currency for most EU nations that lacks a firm institutional foundation. Increasing major-power reliance on bilateral and transactional trade agreements will weaken the World Trade Organization's ability to define and stabilize the economic playing field and compromise the capabilities of crisis-response mechanisms like the International Monetary Fund, the EU's European Stability Mechanism, and the World Bank. Chinese efforts to create alternative global economic institutions through the Asian Infrastructure Investment Fund, the Credit Resources Arrangement (a Chinese-dominated version of the International Monetary Fund), and the Belt and Road initiatives will further erode the Western-led Bretton Woods system.

Sources of Stability and Instability

Virtually by definition, a dysfunctional international system has already achieved a dangerously high level of instability. But all might not be lost. The most important factors in stabilizing and perhaps reversing its deterioration lie in the capabilities and roles played by first- and second-tier nations. If the major powers can contain growing competition among themselves, there is some chance that they will escape the fatalistic predictions of the Thucydides Trap. The Cold War offers one such example: the mutually assured destruction that would almost certainly follow a thermonuclear war convinced the United States and the USSR to find a mutually acceptable relationship through "peaceful coexistence" and deterrence, although regional conflicts such as the Vietnam War or flashpoint confrontations in Cuba and Berlin brought us uncomfortably close to the brink. But such actions require forbearance and a long-term perspective, qualities seldom found in a confrontational and uncertain world.

Second-tier nations could play a two-part role in contributing to stability. First, they could assume greater responsibility for playing peace-keeping and conflict-mediation roles independently of the great powers, contributing in the short run to the stability of the overall system and in the long run building a broader foundation for international cooperation in the future. Their role in stabilizing international and regional institutions also would be critically important, perhaps leading to long-term structural and procedural reforms in the United Nations and other first-tier-dominated bodies. Second, they could resist joining broader military and other alliances built around the growing confrontation of the United States, Russia, and China. To be sure, long-standing historical ties will be difficult to resist. But there is no logic other than history itself to suggest that EU nations should side with the Americans, or that any natural alliance partners exist for Russia or China. While strategic and tactical factors will always be present, there is also a compelling logic to maintaining a degree of flexibility and disengagement.

An unstable multipolar system would find it exceptionally difficult to deal with catastrophic challenges like pandemics, natural disasters, or other upheavals. Overall economic, social, and institutional capabilities would already be diminished by the growing disfunctionality of the system, and increasing conflict across a broad range of issues and at every level of the system would make it difficult to mobilize resources on a global or perhaps even regional basis. The sense of a shared fate would be significantly eroded, if not completely destroyed, and the temptation to pursue individual national goals would be impossible to resist. International or regional institutions would have lost much of their power to the reassertion of aggressive and defiant sovereign nation-states in which domestic political realities would be make it difficult if not impossible to argue for a broader, more cosmopolitan perspective. Each nation's playbook would offer a simple and compelling imperative: our nation first, regardless of the collateral damage. The alliances or other collaborative arrangements that might emerge would be short term, ad hoc, and completely self-serving. The sense of a community of nations, much less of a global system, will have vanished.

Could an Unstable Multipolar World Emerge Today?

Could an unstable multipolar world emerge today? Yes, in a worst-case scenario, and we've already seen it: in the run-up to World War II. The international system created at the Versailles Conference collapsed. The League of Nations failed, in part because of its unrealistic design and in part because of American absence. The United States had returned to its isolationist past, a policy that seemed to serve it well. Germany, Italy, and Japan emerged as revisionist powers. Efforts by Britain, France, and the Soviet Union to form an effective alliance failed, largely from mutual distrust and the unwillingness of smaller European powers to play their role. The Soviet Union was held at arm's length for most of the period, viewed as a revolutionary and revisionist state and denied participation in the League of Nations until it was too late. Secondary conflicts such as the Spanish Civil War became testing grounds for major powers like Germany, and little was done to end the fighting. The Japanese invasion of Manchuria in 1931 resulted in the creation of a puppet state, Manchukuo, on the Chinese mainland. Throughout Europe, the democracies created after World War I fell victim to instability, most eventually toppled by right-wing or military coups. After the U.S. stock market crash in 1929, economic failure spread across the continent, destroying public confidence in the new democracies and spawning social and political unrest. The "war to end all wars" had ended nothing, as Europe and eventually most of the world fell victim to the failure of well-meaning but naïve efforts to create a new international system.

NOTES

1. Henry A. Kissinger, *World Order* (Penguin, 2014), 3.

2. Niccolo Machiavelli, *The Prince* (University of Chicago Press, 1998). Originally published in 1532.

3. Comments to the House of Commons, March 1, 1848.

4. Robert Keohane, *After Hegemony: Cooperation and Discord in the World Political Economy* (Princeton University Press, 1984).

5. George Modelski, *Long Cycles in World Politics* (Palgrave, 1987).

6. A. F. K. Organski, *World Politics* (Knopf, 1958).

7. Graham Allison, *Destined for War: Can America and China Escape Thucydides's Trap?* (Houghton Mifflin Harcourt, 2017).

8. Michael Mandelbaum, *Mission Failure: America and the World in the Post-Cold War Era* (Oxford University Press, 2016).

9. Deborah Welsh Larson and Alexei Shevchenko, *The Quest for Status: Chinese and Russian Foreign Policy* (Yale University Press, 2019); Elizabeth Economy, *The Third Revolution: Xi Jinping and the New Chinese State* (Oxford University Press, 2018); and Donald R. Kelley, *Russian Politics and Presidential Power: Transformational Leadership from Gorbachev to Putin* (CQ/SAGE, 2017).

10. John Lewis Gaddis, *The Cold War: A New History* (Penguin, 2016); and Odd Arne Westad, *The Cold War: A World History* (Basic Books, 2017).

11. Seth Johnson, *How NATO Adapts: Strategy and Organization in the Atlantic Alliance since 1950* (Johns Hopkins University Press, 2017); Neil Fodor, *The Warsaw Treaty Organization: A Political and Organizational Analysis* (Palgrave Macmillan, 1990); and Dimitar Bechev, *Rival Power: Russia's Influence in Southeast Europe* (Yale University Press, 2017).

12. Barbara W. Tuchman and Robert K. Massie, *The Guns of August* (Presidio, 2004).

13. Fareed Zakaria, *The Post-American World* (Norton, 2009), 1–5.

14. United Nations, http://www.un.org./en/member-states/.

15. *U.S. News and World Report*, "Power Ranking," http://www.usnews.com/news/best-countries/power-rankings.

16. Investopia, "The Top 20 Economies in the World," http://www.investopia.com/insights/worlds-top-economies/, August 16, 2018.

17. Global Firepower, "2018 Military Strength Rankings," http://www.globalfirepower.com/countrylistings, 2020.

18. Portland Communication and USC Center for Public Diplomacy, "Soft Power," *Fortune*, July 13, 2019.

19. *Newsweek*, http://www.newsweek.com/what-countries-have-nuclear-weapons; CNBC, http://www.cnbc.com/2018/03/16/list-of-countries-with-nuclear-weapons.

20. Peter Hajnal, "The G 8 System and the G 20: Evolution, Role, and Documentation," *Global Finance Series* (Ashgate, 2007).

3

The Economic Paradigm

THE PARADIGM

The role of economic factors becomes increasingly important in the international system, initially reshaping the relationships established by the nation-state paradigm and eventually challenging their role as the most important determinants of the global pecking order among nation-states, economic blocs, international organizations, and multinational actors.

A few caveats are important. First, the nation-state as we know it will remain an essential component of the international system. There will still be countries, governments, and a sense of national identity. But the economic paradigm tells us that they will be different, transformed internally by their nation's involvement in an increasingly interconnected world.

Second, it will all be very controversial. Economic decisions are also political decisions, and vice versa. There will be winners and losers, although it may take a very long time to sort out which is which. At the end of World War II, there was a widespread consensus that creating the Bretton Woods system to encourage free trade and economic interdependence would eventually produce a world in which war was less likely. But there also were a number of unexpected consequences that in today's world have produced conflicts within and among nations and a growing skepticism about the underlying arguments for globalization and free trade.

Third, there are many competing economic paradigms that claim to tell us how the world works and where it is headed. As we said in chapter 1, academic disciplines aren't paradigms; they just tell us where to look for answers. Paradigms are more specific, like "capitalism," or "socialism," or in the case of international economics, "comparative advantage," "free trade," "mercantilism," "neomercantilism," and "mercantilism 2.0," the latter invented for our purposes in this book. It gets confusing. . . .

To deal with that confusion, let's look quickly at what an economic paradigm tells us. All of them deal with the same issues. What are the most important resources that shape the economy? Is it land, as in an economy based on agriculture? Is it capital, an economist's generic term for financial wealth or other resources than can be invested for economic gain. Is it technology? Economists tell us that there have been four, or maybe five, industrial revolutions. The first began in Britain in the late eighteenth century and spread throughout the world; the second, sometimes called the "technological revolution," began in the late nineteenth and early twentieth centuries and was marked by fundamental technical revolutions and the advent of mass production; the third, based on the impact of computerization, automation, and high technology, began in the mid-twentieth century; and the fourth began at the end of the twentieth and beginning of the twenty-first centuries, based on even more advanced technology in computers, robotics, nanotechnology, and artificial intelligence. Some analysts argue that we are on the cusp of a fifth industrial revolution, based on the interaction of artificial intelligence and biological technologies, its implications not fully known.[1]

Economic paradigms are about more than just resources and technology. They also are social models that tell us about who owns and/or controls these resources, how economic and political decisions about these issues are made, and how the wealth generated by these resources is distributed. They are about who wins and who loses, which puts them at the core of human conflict within and among nations.

Three different economic paradigms are relevant to our discussion of how the international system might evolve in the future: classical mercantilism, comparative advantage (also sometimes called "liberalism" or the "free trade" model), and neomercantilism.

Classical Mercantilism

Classical mercantilism is the economic theory of empires, dominant in Europe from the sixteenth to the late nineteenth centuries, although the empires for which it provided the theoretical justification survived until the middle of the twentieth century. At its core, mercantilism is about increasing the power of the state. While wealth was largely privately held, the state exercised extensive control over economic policy and trade to enrich the nation. Colonial empires were designed to further that end. Trade with the colonies was to benefit the mother country, providing raw materials, outsourced labor, and eventually markets. Protective tariffs and other trade barriers were designed to create a positive trade balance (meaning that the mother country exported more than it imported) and to protect fledgling home industries against foreign competition. And throughout the process, the growing power of the state was used to increase government revenues through taxes, tariffs, and other mechanisms. As Adam Smith insightfully put it in the title of his 1776 book *The Wealth of Nations*, it was about the wealth of *nations*, not producers or consumers.[2]

Comparative Advantage

The theory of comparative advantage argues that each producer should specialize in those products that he or she produces most efficiently (meaning maximum output for minimum input of resources) and trade with someone else to buy those things that the other producer can make more efficiently. In other words, do what you're best at, and to get those things you don't produce efficiently, trade with someone else who is best at making those things. People in Idaho shouldn't try to grow oranges and grapefruit, and people in Florida shouldn't try to grow potatoes. Create a marketplace in which each can buy the other's output. Simple. Everybody wins, at least in theory. The economists are happy because on the whole the economy isn't wasting resources; the producers are happy because they get to sell the things they are best at producing at the lowest cost; and the consumers are happy because they have a broader assortment of choices at the lowest possible price.

What's the role of the state? To create and regulate the marketplace so that free trade can occur to the mutual advantage of all producers and consumers. That's all—just get out of the way of a logical mechanism that gives people more for less. Virtually all nation-states have created such an open market that encompasses all of their own territory; potato-loving Floridians don't pay a tariff on Idaho-grown potatoes, and grapefruit-loving Idahoans don't pay a tariff on Florida's citrus fruit. In the real world, it is more complex, of course, but the central premise of the argument became the rallying cry for advocates of free trade, especially as support for tightly restrictive mercantilist trade patterns began to ebb in the first half of the twentieth century.

The first half of the twentieth century also witnessed two world wars and a worldwide economic depression after the 1929 crash of the U.S stock market. Desperate to avoid a repeat performance, the creators of the Bretton Woods system sought to mobilize the economic logic of comparative advantage to political ends: *if* free trade would foster the interdependence of former enemies, especially in Europe; *if* new economic and political institutions such as the Common Market and its eventual successor, the European Union, could change the political landscape of the continent; *if* these successes could draw other powerful nations, especially the United States, into a growing global economy, building a strong bastion against the spread of communism and eventually an alternative model for the communist giants, *then* perhaps they could create a new international system increasingly defined and motivated by economics rather than the traditional nation-state model.[3]

Neomercantilism

The term *neomercantilism* has been used to describe several different things in the post–World War II world. Its greatest impact, at least until recently, has been what we choose to call *developmental* neomercantilism.

It describes a model for economic development for nations trying to catch up with the rest of the world, especially in terms of industrialization and successful entry into a global economy. Simply put, these nations are playing catch-up, starting at a disadvantage perhaps because they are former colonies exploited by the colonial power, perhaps because they initially followed the wrong model for economic success (the Soviet Union and Eastern Europe after the fall of communism in 1991, or China after Deng Xiaoping's market reforms in the 1980s), or perhaps because they are just extremely poor. The strategy is an accelerated version of the mercantilism that worked well for the world's first industrial powers. The government plays a central and controlling role in identifying what resources the nation may have to exploit, usually cheap labor or exportable natural resources or agricultural products. Whatever it is, it is ruthlessly exploited to establish a niche in the larger world economy. The growth of the economy becomes export driven, and the profits are invested (under strong governmental guidance) to raise the technological sophistication and diversification of the economy. Soon a nation, once known for Happy Meal toys, Christmas ornaments, and shoddy knock-offs of upscale merchandise, is exporting cell phones and computers and capturing increasing global market share.

More is required. Neomercantilist economies also resort to classical protectionist measures. Local industries are protected against foreign competition by high tariffs or other trade restrictions. Currency manipulation frequently occurs, making the domestic currency cheap to foreign buyers as a way to encourage exports. Domestic consumers are encouraged to buy domestically made products. Despite the seemingly ubiquitous presence of McDonald's and Walmart, these economies remain relatively closed in comparison to their more globalized counterparts. And so it goes, with remarkable success for many of the world's emerging market economies and current and future economic giants like Japan, China, and South Korea, to name a few among many.

At least in theory, developmental neomercantilism is supposed to be a temporary phase that lets late-starters catch up with more advanced economies. It gives them short-term advantages that should be given up when they are sufficiently developed to play the game of international trade by the same rules as their already more advanced counterparts. Simply put, they get a break, at least for a while, in part because they are starting out at some disadvantage and in part because the rest of the world will eventually benefit from their successful integration into a global economy. But problems can arise. When does a developmental neomercantilist nation "graduate" and go out on its own? "Now" or "It should have already happened," is the answer given by the more developed nations that are tired of tolerating the special status accorded to such nations. "Not yet" or "When we're ready," respond the developing nations, anxious to hold on to their advantaged status as long as possible. There is no clear answer, other than to say that it becomes an increasingly divisive issue that is at the core of understanding how changing economic realities shape the debate about the future of the international system.[4]

The economic paradigm posits:

- **Economic power is the most important measure of national power and an increasingly significant factor in the definition of "national interest."**

Any assessment of a nation's economic power usually begins with a discussion of its gross domestic product (GDP, a monetary measure of the market value of all final goods and services produced in a country). While it gives you the best overall comparative measure of how much a country produces, it is not a full picture of a nation's economic power in the real world. Additional measures are required to give the full picture.

Vitally important is an assessment of how that wealth is used. A common measure is the nation's military budget, but it doesn't tell us everything. How much does the nation spend to sustain its military power, and how does that compare with other nations? What percentage of the nation's total GDP is spent on the military, and how is that divided among the army, navy, air force or between conventional or nuclear forces or between offensive and defensive capabilities? How much is spent on research and development, especially on cutting-edge technology? How much goes to other elements of national defense, such as the intelligence and diplomatic services?

In a broader social context, how much of the national wealth goes to a higher standard of living, to increased consumer purchasing power, or to the creation of a network of public services such as education and health care, all important in creating a sense of performance legitimacy, and social and political stability within the nation?

Economic issues also become an increasingly important element in determining the country's "national interest." Any assessment of a nation's vulnerabilities and opportunities now includes the impact that other nations' economic decisions have on it and how its decisions impact others. Economic interdependence cuts both ways; what we do affects others, and what others do affects us.

- **Significant economic and institutional changes occur within and among nations that have broad political, social, cultural, and distributional implications.**

Who you are, what you produce, how you produce it, from whom you buy it or to whom you sell it, and who wins or loses are all redefined, gradually at first but with cumulative and far-reaching impact. Things were once simpler, or so they seemed. You were once a French dairy farmer, but now you're also a citizen of the EU and a part of an international system of supply chains. Or perhaps you're an American farmer who depends on soybean exports, or a worker in a Chrysler auto factory who now is a part of global supply chain bringing auto parts from other countries to be assembled into an automobile in your factory that eventually will be sold to an international market (and by the way, it's now Fiat-Chrysler-Peugeot, the result of an Italian-American-French merger).

- **The number and character of economically relevant actors expands, still including traditional nation-states but expanding** to encompass non-state actors such as multinational corporations (MNCs); large and nearly global trade regimes such as the World Trade Organization (WTO); regional trading blocs such as the EU and the USMCA (formerly NAFTA); the Bretton Woods entities such as the International Monetary Fund (IMF), the World Bank, and the WTO, transformed over time but still central to the operation of the international economy; and a growing number of international trade and business associations representing specific sectors of the economy (the Organization of Petroleum Exporting Countries [OPEC], among many others).

Simply put, everything is getting more complex, befitting the growth of the global economy itself but also signaling the emergence of a more complex set of institutional and political relationships that produce both cooperation and conflict. Let's remember one of the basic facts of the post–World War II world: the United Nations grew from 51 to 193 members, with virtually all involved in some way with international economic issues. The WTO has 164 members and 12 "observer governments." Virtually all of the support and regulatory agencies involved in the expansion of international trade have grown apace, including the international banking system; the legal services needed to complete commercial transactions; the agencies that standardize the technical details of production to be sure that a cell phone using U.S.-made chips and assembled in China will perform perfectly in the hands of a French consumer; the transportation networks needed move merchandise from the factory to the consumer; the network of wholesale middlemen through which merchandise passes; and more, much more. Collectively known as "supply chains," they encompass the complex realties of a global economy, orchestrating a level of interaction and production never before seen when they perform well but potentially foretelling the collapse of a well-oiled machine if they fall victim to accidental or purposeful disruption, as the economic impact of the COVID-19 pandemic has quickly taught us.

That brings us to another reality about the institutions that serve the global economy: they all operate within a complex and conflicted political milieu. They have their own sense of institutional identity and mission: to promote international trade if you're the WTO, to facilitate the day-to-day flow of trade if you're an international banker or lawyer, to promote economic stability if you're the IMF, and so on. But it doesn't end with that narrow sense of institutional identity. Does it matter whether you are a French or a German banker, especially if you work within the context of the European Union? Or does the economic well-being of your own country come ahead of your commitment to free trade or the rules of the WTO? Not easy, is it? Political scientists describe this as the dilemma of overlapping identities and institutional loyalties, but that doesn't make it any easier to solve. In the end, it's a political choice, one that shapes how you think about the many different possible futures of the international system.

- **The economic paradigm conceptualizes the future of the international system in terms of how economic changes occurring within and among states transform the international system, creating new and conflicted economic and institutional realities that increasingly transcend traditional nation-state boundaries, identities and cultures, and ideologies.**

The outcome will not be a simple winner-take-all victory. New economic realities will transform the nation-state, but the enduring and deeply rooted sense of nation-states, identities and cultures, and ideologies will shape how economic changes take form in the real world. The result will be a synthesis combining elements from all perspectives. It won't be a universally accepted or stable synthesis, at least for a while. It will be different from place to place, and it will change over time. And it will be deeply controversial, placing it at the center of bitter and probably sometimes violent struggles within and among nations.

THE POSSIBLE FUTURES

When viewed from the perspective of the economic paradigm, several possible alternative futures emerge (see table 3.1). They include:

- **globalization advances,** built around the increasing scope and depth of economic interdependence and free trade;

- **globalization amended or transformed,** built around a number of possible institutional and political arrangements that preserve the core of a global or regional economy while maintaining a significant role for nation-states;

- **mercantilism 2.0,** built around the emergence of assertive nation-states eager to place the prosperity of their country ahead of others and willing to substantially alter the institutional structures of a global economy; and

- **toward autarky (and anarchy),** a worst-case scenario built around economic crises and possible collapse within all but the strongest economies and a precipitous decline in international trade.

Table 3.1. The Economic Paradigm

Globalization Advances	Globalization, Amended and Reconfigured	Mercantilism 2.0	Toward Autarky, with a Touch of Anarchy
Hierarchy and power are determined by a nation's economic capabilities, trade, and technology	Opposition to globalization causes some nations to take greater control over their economies	Economic nationalism increases, and nations turn inward and reduce global commitments	The number of Mercantilism 2.0 nations increases, increasing global competition

Table 3.1 (*cont.*)

Globalization Advances	Globalization, Amended and Reconfigured	Mercantilism 2.0	Toward Autarky, with a Touch of Anarchy
Global and regional trade regimes shape the international system	Growing economic rivalry stokes political conflict among nations	The power of global and regional trade regimes decreases, leading to ad hoc and bilateral arrangements	Nations prioritize their own interests and rely less on existing trade regimes
Nations become more interdependent, based on supply chains and mobility of labor, capital, and technology	Trade regimes are reconfigured to play a continuing but reduced role	Declining economic ties lead to a reduction of commitments to other international bodies and agreements	Major powers abandon leadership roles and turn inward
Nations sort themselves into hierarchies such as the G-7 and G-20	Bilateral and ad hoc agreement play a greater role	Competition among first-tier nations grows, and second- and third-tier nations complete for local or regional power	The global infrastructure atrophies or collapses
Globalization causes economic, political, and social change within nations	Interdependence decreases but does not cease to occur		First-tier nations aspire to hegemonic status, second- and third-tier nations seek regional dominance

Globalization Advances

The trade patterns associated with globalization widen and deepen, involving more nations and encompassing a broader scope of economic activity in all sectors of the economy, most importantly manufacturing, services, and high-tech sectors in artificial intelligence, big data analytics, nanotechnology, and bioengineering. Formalized trade regimes become more powerful and invasive, deepening the impact of a rule-based system of international trade. Supply chains grow more complex, and the economies they serve grow more interdependent at all levels of production and consumption. Overall trade levels increase, but not at the rate of growth seen in the initial phases of globalization in the 1980s. Institutions such as the World Trade Organization grow more important in facilitating trade and mediating disputes, and regional organizations such as the EU, in which globalization experienced its first successes in the post–World War II era, remain important in bridging the gap between truly global and regional trade patterns. The economic superpowers continue to play a key role, but the ranks of second-tier nations grow, expanding the G-20 into the G-20+ and enlarging the membership and diversity of similar bodies. Developmental neomercantilism remains a viable growth strategy, and nations willingly "graduate" to full membership in a global economy.[5]

Advancing globalization will have its limits and problems. It does not signal the beginning of a utopia or the first stages of a world government. Nation-states will remain essential actors, their role transformed but not ended by advancing globalization. Conflicts will continue, and some will intensify as a nation's economic power and well-being become entangled in a complex web of global dependencies and rivalries. Globalism will cut both ways, both making nations increasingly sensitive to the economic policies of others and simultaneously making it costly to let rivalries spill over into armed conflicts.

Continuing globalization will also exact economic, social, and political costs. There will be winners and losers. Workers in some countries will prosper and get jobs in new high-tech industries, while others will lose by the same measure. Opposition to globalization will grow, producing demands for change or compensation or, at the least, acknowledgment that some have fallen behind. Such opposition will find its voice through protest movements (the Yellow Vests in France and the now common-place protests at G-7, G-20, and WTO meetings), political parties (the Brexit Party in Great Britain, National Rally in France, Alternative for Germany, League in Italy, and Sweden Democrats), and charismatic politicians (Marine Le Pen in France, Matteo Salvini in Italy, and Donald Trump in the United States).

The Structure of Advancing Globalization

In many ways, there will be little initial formal structural change in a world marked by advancing globalization. As we've said, nation-states and the major institutional players will remain the same, functioning on a broader scale in support of increasing trade. What will change is the broader political and social milieu within which they operate, creating greater national and institutional commitment to and public confidence in the benefits of increasing global interdependence.

That said, there will be limited change in the institutional structure of world trade. As they have done before, institutions created through the Bretton Woods agreement will further evolve.[6] The WTO will play an even more significant role in setting the terms of international exchanges and mediating disputes. Other organizations like the IMF and the World Bank will become more effective, as will a growing assortment of formal and informal mechanisms designed for crisis management and the con-tinued development of third- or fourth-tier economies. Broad acceptance of the developmental neomercantilism model of economic development will continue, justified by the "graduation" of now advanced nations like China or South Korea. Negotiations to continue further tariff reduc-tions, now stalled in the deadlock of the Doha Round of WTO talks, may resume and begin to resolve the difficult issues of agricultural trade and intellectual property, which have stalled the talks for over a decade. Regional trading blocs will be strengthened or created in areas where they do not exist, and bloc-to-bloc trade will grow. Multinational corporations will grow in size and depth, uniting similar sectors across nations and continents (the emergence of the global auto giants Volkswagen-Ford or Fiat-Chrysler-Peugeot are examples of a growing trend that is now expanding into the high technology, telecommunications, entertainment, and retailing sectors).

Also important is the increasing acceptance of a sense of global culture, defined more in terms of consumerism and a common sense of how we want to live and what we want to consume than in terms of broader political, religious, or ideological beliefs. It's about more than the physical exchange of merchandise. It's about what those exchanges bring before us every day that becomes a part of our self-definition—news, entertainment, lifestyle and consumption choices, perceptions of the wide range of possibilities that are within our grasp—all of those things that offer a globalized menu of what is possible and what seems desirable. An increasingly globalized economy creates and ultimately requires globalized consumers.[7]

How Power Is Distributed in Advancing Globalization

As globalization advances, power will gradually shift from individual nation-states toward rule-based multilateral entities, regulatory and process-setting agencies, and transnational nongovernmental entitles, including increasingly important multinational corporations and trade groups. In simpler terms, international trade will become less "political" and more driven by market decisions, occurring within an increasingly complex and invasive institutional context in which multilateral and multinational agencies will encourage, facilitate, regulate, and adjudicate the ebb and flow of trade, all based on a set of commonly accepted rules that governments set in place through the creation of "trade regimes." To be sure, the creation of the "regimes"—just another word for trade agreements like the original Common Market and European Economic Community, the United States-Mexico-Canada Agreement, or the World Trade Organization—was intensely political and the subject of contentious negotiations among the member countries, and from time to time, member states reasserted their prerogatives and demanded modification to reflect new realities. But once in place, the regimes provide most of the rules that tell us how to trade with one another on a day-to-day basis and how to deal with frequent but not system-challenging disputes. We know the rules of the game, we have the playbook, and for most of us, the benefits of playing by the rules exceed the costs.[8]

Sources of Stability and Instability in Advancing Globalization

Stability or potential instability will be linked to both economic and political factors. In economic terms, stability will depend on the management of market fluctuations and occasional crises. Markets will go up and down as they always do, and events in one part of the world will have an impact around the globe. "Bubbles" will burst, producing boom-and-bust cycles that impact markets. Currency exchange rates will fluctuate, usually signaling short-term shifts but sometimes indicating more fundamental assessments of an economy's future prospects. Special cases, like the euro, will have greater impact across the imperfectly institutionalized banking and currency system of the EU.[9]

Stability also will be affected by the perceived overall success of globalization. Has it continued to produce "prosperity," however defined, at acceptable social and political costs? For most people in most places, do things still seem to be getting better? Is international trade continuing to expand and deepen, albeit perhaps at a decreasing growth rate because globalization is reaching a point of diminishing returns? Are emerging economies "graduating" from the developmental neomercantiilist transition phase and taking their rightful place in the global economy?

Political considerations also will impact on the stability or instability of advancing globalization. If the answer to most of the questions posed above is "no," then political problems will quickly follow. If those answers seem to say "It isn't working as well as it once did" or "It never worked for us," then there will be growing demands to slow or roll back globalization. The proposed solutions will include: ending broadly inclusive trade regimes like the WTO or the EU and returning to ad hoc one-to-one or smaller agreements; fixing the system by amending and reconfiguring globalization (discussed in the next section); or shifting to a new sort of mercantilism 2.0 (discussed in the section after the next), and evoking a sense of "my country first."

Responses to catastrophic challenges such as pandemics, natural disasters, or other shocks to the system also will be shaped by economic and political factors. Such events are likely to reduce overall economic resources on a global scale, exacerbating the differences between rich and poor nations and compromising the resources available to international bodies that attempt to respond. Even the nations initially most committed to multilateral responses will be tempted to turn inward to care for their own citizens or allies, responding to growing political pressures for crisis-related and perhaps long-term adjustments to their once expanding global or regional roles. Such crises are also likely to create new political wedge issues within and among nations that would challenge the preexisting consensus that sustained globalization. They also may fundamentally alter the very nature of the international economy itself. The economic impact of the COVID-19 pandemic had far-reaching and largely unanticipated consequences across the globe, disrupting smoothly operating supply chains in ways that quickly reached from Wall Street and other global financial centers to the Main Streets and back streets of the world. The dominos fell more quickly than anyone thought possible, and no one is sure of how or when, or perhaps even if, a new and more stable order will emerge.

What Would It Be Like If We Lived in a World of Advancing Globalization?

It's not today's world, at least in the short run. The widespread and unquestioning acceptance of the theory of comparative advantage, on which free trade is based, the dynamic growth of globalization through trading blocs like the EU, and the rapid export-driven success of Japan and China in the 1970s and 1980s now seem a thing of the past. Perhaps they have run their course, creating a world in which the very success of free trade and globalization has spawned opposition to its further expansion. The overall success of early globalization was premised on the nature of the post–World War II world, adjusted to deal with the Cold War. That world is gone, and there is no commonly accepted view of what will take its place. Where the major powers like the United States, China, and Russia will fit in is unclear and contentious, and the list of increasingly powerful countries, such as the G-20 members who want a seat at the table, is growing. Issues like global warming and climate change, environmental destruction, migration, human rights, and others will also be a part of the debate, and no one nation or small group of nations, economic blocs, or international institutions like the UN will control the discussion. The once-shared playbook that told us how to interact in even the most conflicted times now seems to have multiple editions or revisions; most of the time, most of the players follow most of the rules, but not always. And if the major powers—the United States, China, Russia, and the EU—strike out of their own, admittedly for reasons that seem wise and fair to them, then a world of advancing globalization will become a world of growing and uncertain conflict.

GLOBALIZATION AMENDED AND RECONFIGURED

Globalization has been amended and reconfigured—but not abandoned—at least in the sense that the changes attempt to preserve as much of the benefits of free trade as possible while making the economic, institutional, and political adjustments needed to avoid a complete backlash against globalization. It will not be a single paradigm, accepted by all players. Rather it will be a series of economic and political compromises, changing over time in response to the realities of the moment. It will involve changes *within* nations, as their economies modernize and prosper or fall behind and languish, and as their political leaders sort out who reaps the benefits or bears the costs. It will be change in the economic and political relationships *among* nations, as they compete for power within multilateral institutions such as the WTO, regional trade blocs, and the broader international arena. How it happens also will be a matter of considerable

disagreement. Will the existing institutional order be peacefully transformed through a series of regional or global negotiations, and if so, who
will take the lead? Or will change require some degree of disruption, a
shock to the system in both political and economic terms, led by major
players who unilaterally take bold action to change the institutions and
the playbook?

Whatever the answer, such change will take place within the larger
context of a changing international system. The starting point is an already
complex and conflicted world, shaped by:

- the post–Cold War reemergence of superpower rivalries between
  the United States, Russia, and China;

- major changes in many of the formal institutions of global or
  regional trade (the WTO, NAFTA, and the EU, to cite the most
  obvious examples) and not-yet-clear revisions to the informal
  playbook that tells us how to play the game;

- rising demands for some form of compensation to deal with
  the social and political impact of global trade (bilateral trade
  agreements to even out import-export inequities, the protection of
  jobs or retraining programs for nations suffering from outsourced
  production, or restrictions on immigration policies that had led to
  an influx of foreign workers, and so on);

- growing political instability in long-standing democracies like
  Great Britain, France, and the United States, and authoritarian
  challenges to newer democracies like Russia, Hungary, or Poland,
  some but not all of it linked to the impact of economic change; and

- growing concern about issues not easily fitting into the geopolitical
  or economic worldviews that have dominated the post–World War
  II world, especially global warming, climate change, human rights,
  and international migration, or the impact of shocks to the system
  like the COVID-19 pandemic.

The Structure of Globalization Amended and Reconfigured

"Structures" of globalization is probably more correct than "structure." By definition, the international system is in flux, searching for the best of all possible compromises between those who want to advance globalization and those who want rein it in or do away with it. There are no clearly articulated or accepted alternatives, no black or white dichotomous choices. The list of major players remains essentially the same: nation-states at different levels of economic development and with differing and potentially conflicting goals, aspirations, and fears; a host of trade-related multilateral entities, including the contemporary versions of the initial Bretton Woods system, now joined by regional trade blocs, and other new entities created to supplement or to challenge the Bretton Woods institutions; a growing number of ad hoc, usually bilateral trade agreements; and, in the private sector, increasingly powerful MNCs and resource-related cartels like the OPEC.

What makes the structure increasingly complex and conflicted is that the line-ups are no longer clear. Each actor will play different roles at different times, dictated by its position in the global economy and historical commitments to the Bretton Woods system but also by its short-term economic, social, and domestic political concerns. The ambiguity is clearest and most disruptive among the major nation-states. The United States, once seen as one of the bedrock nations defending the international economic order, has shifted away from globalization toward what the next section will call "neomercantilism 2.0," a form of economic nationalism and protectionism—but not completely or irreversibly, at least so far.[10] Trade agreements are altered by direct bilateral pacts or "amended" or "renegotiated," with no clear overall template in place, except for the general perception that the existing arrangements are somehow unfair and the realization that economic nationalism is politically popular. Great Britain's raucous departure from the EU marks a similar pattern; London first hoped that it could have it both ways, breaking political and social policy ties, especially concerning the movement of EU citizens within the bloc, while selectively preserving mutually beneficial trade relations.[11]

China, too, touts its own version of globalization, framed by its increasingly inappropriate status as an advanced economy still advantaged by aspects of its former neomercantilist position, which included access to foreign markets for its exports but protection of its own economy through import limitations, subsidies to domestic producers, and currency manipulation.[12] Japan's export-driven economy evidences a similar contradiction, benefiting from its penetration of foreign markets while protecting its own domestic industries and agricultural producers.[13] Other nations have their own unique positions. France remains a staunch advocate of global and regional trade, but links both to further European economic and political integration. Germany continues to support inclusive global and regional trade arrangements, but seeks to impose its own version of fiscal conservatism on the EU. In both nations, pro-trade positions are increasingly challenged by the rise of right-wing populist parties. And on it goes, the point being that nations do not line up consistently on one side of the issue of globalization. Confusing, as befits the modern world, but understandable, given the complex political, social, and economic realities they face.[14]

The institutional structure that emerged in connection with the Bretton Woods system has also played an important but increasingly conflicted role. The WTO, IMF, and World Bank have faced increasing difficulties in trying to play their designated roles. For the WTO, the task has been twofold: to encourage the removal of remaining trade restrictions, a task now hopelessly deadlocked with the stalemate of the current Doha Round of negotiations, and to regulate and adjudicate trade disputes in an increasingly complex and litigious global trading community. Neither task is easy, and the WTO's track record in recent years has been mixed at best, more a product of existential political and economic realities than an inherent shortcoming of the institution itself. The same is true for the IMF, whose stabilization mission has been complicated by the increasing scope and cost of economic crises, now measured in terms of their impact on regional trading blocs like the EU or large sectors of the global economy rather than by the fate of a particular nation's economy. While help has come from the creation of new bodies like the EU's Economic Stabilization Mechanism, the threat remains that regional or global economic failures could overwhelm the system. Also potentially helpful, but with a significant political price, is the creation of Chinese-led initiatives, such as the Belt and Road projects to link China and Europe more closely, and the Asian Infrastructure Development Bank, which is seen as an effort to create a Chinese-dominated version of an alternative Bretton Woods system for the twenty-first century.

Also significant is the growing role of private-sector or jointly private–state owned entities that make up many of the world's most powerful MNCs. Examples include Exxon Mobil, Microsoft, Alphabet, Google, Royal Dutch Shell, Saudi Aramco, Apple, Bank of America, China Mobile, General Electric, Amazon, and many more. At one level, most endorse continued or enlarged globalization as economically beneficial to themselves; the bigger they are, the bigger their capital and technology needs, the more complex their multinational supply chains, and the larger their potential customer base. But economic and political realities also shape their policies. Maintaining market share, protecting access to raw materials and technology, and protecting domestic markets while prying open foreign ones (to say nothing of the impact of government influence) cannot but compromise even the purest theoretical commitment to free trade.[15]

The Distribution of Power in Globalization Amended and Reconfigured

Consistent with the growing complexity of an amended and reconfigured globalist world, power is more widely distributed within the international system. Given the growing lack of consensus on the structure and functioning of a global economy, the playing field becomes more contentious and conflicted. Issues that were once regarded as already decided and institutionalized through formal agreements and the mutual understandings that made up the playbook are now open to conflict and reinterpretation. Nation-states eager to revise the rules of the game challenge what had been accepted conventional wisdom, reinterpreting or outright breaking the rules and finding new economic and political weapons with which to challenge the system.

Any assessment of the distribution of power in a changing global economy also must deal with the question "power to do what?" Faced with growing demands for change, the system now is shaped by two different kinds of power. The first is the power to largely maintain the status quo. Nations, institutions, and private-sector entities usually prefer to remain within their own comfort zones; the system seems to work well, at least for them, and it is backstopped by a network of other economic, political, social, and cultural connections built over time. Changing any part of a network potentially places all of the others at some risk. Economic change spills over to affect other elements of foreign and defense policy or a host of other "special relationships" that define the world as we know it. The temptation to resist change is seductive. It's easier to ignore or postpone an issue, to kick the can down the road, and to let political and institutional inertia treat it as business as usual. Easy also to find short-term fixes or "work-arounds," ad hoc informal arrangements that may deal with the political issues at the expense of sidestepping the real substantive problems. It's what governments and especially bureaucracies are good at, and it seems to solve the problem, at least for a while.

But in the world of amended and reconfigured globalization, there is a second kind of power: the power to force change, to disrupt the system, and to break the rules or make your own rules. Not everybody has it. The bedrock institutions like the WTO, IMF, and World Bank, and the regional trading blocs like the EU and USMCA are locked into their institutionalized roles, and most nation-states simply don't have the economic, military, or diplomatic clout to force change.

But some do, and their ability to force change in the face of institutional inertia and widespread opposition marks them as the disruptors of the old order and the possible creators of the new. It's happened before, as the Bretton Woods system and the evolution of the Common Market into the European Union shaped the modern world. At the time of their creation, they were experimental and controversial, and certainly not sure of success. The same thing is happening today. Already a significant economic and a growing military power, China is aggressively trying to take greater control of how it deals economically with the rest of the world: from the global impact of the Belt and Road projects and the creation of an array of international economic institutions such as the Asia Infrastructure Development Bank as a potential counterweight to Bretton Woods, to the micromanagement of how Chinese corporations deal with others in terms of joint projects, access to domestic markets, and technology acquisition. As noted earlier, Great Britain's withdrawal from the EU was at its core an attempt to compel Brussels to accept change on London's terms, albeit it change that went badly askew.

Seen in this context, American efforts, especially since the election of Donald Trump, are similar, if more aggressive, attempts to redefine but not do away with the global economic order in ways that serve American interests. None of the issues is really new; the relative decline of American economic power, outsourcing of jobs to cheap labor markets, influx of foreign-produced goods to American stores, globalization of capital and technology markets, and broader social and political impact of all of the above have been there for a long time. What is new, and to many disruptive and wrongheaded and to others bold and innovative, are the tactics being used to deal with the issues. They are the first steps toward what in the next section is labeled "coercive transactionalism," a policy in which a powerful nation uses its economic power to coerce its trading partners to alter their behavior in ways favorable to it. It's bold, innovative, and disruptive. It breaks some but not all of the formal rules and informal understandings developed in a gentler and more rule-governed world. Unilateral initiatives rather than action through multilateral entities such as the WTO or other formal trade regimes are increasingly common, as is linkage between economic levers and issues that seemingly have little to do directly with trade issues per se (the threat of economic sanctions against Mexico as leverage to force it to limit the passage of asylum seekers toward the U.S.-Mexican border, for example). Coercive transactionalism also frequently entails the forced revision of existing trade pacts, especially on a bilateral basis; the withdrawal or threat of withdrawal from international bodies as leverage to forward the American agenda (the United States threatened to withdraw from the International Postal Organization, one of the oldest and most benign multilateral bodies, as leverage to force revisions on how the agency treats China); and the weaponization of tariffs, non-tariff trade barriers, and economic sanctions on individuals, specific corporations such as Huawei, and financial organizations. These actions are controversial, evoking deep support and raging condemnation. They are experimental, and the success of a tool like tariffs may lead to their indiscriminate application in less appropriate venues. They are templates that can be copied by other nations, at first as a quid pro quo to counter American actions and later as a proven strategy that may be employed at a nation's discretion.

Sources of Stability and Instability in Globalization Amended and Reconfigured

By definition, a system defined as being "amended and reconfigured" faces some level of built-in instability. The question is how much, and why is it there? If the intent of the major revisionist powers is to "fix" the system—maintain a high level of global trade while solving whatever problems have emerged—then whatever stress emerges can be managed in the long run, even though the short-term impact may be jarring. If the intent is to fundamentally redesign the system, change the formal institutions and informal playbooks, and realign the list of winners and losers, then the impact will be far greater. And if the answer in the real world is that some revisionists want little "fixes" and others want a fundamental "big fix," the stability of a transitional system will be up for grabs. China and Great Britain seem at present to belong to the "big fix" category, while the United States vacillates between sweeping initial demands for change (the "big fix") and acceptance of lesser, compromise outcomes (the "little fix"), frequently rebranded as major changes. France and Germany fall into the "little fix" category, the former opting for a modest deepening of the EU experience, and the latter calling for better management of the existing order. Russia is a wildcard, demanding recognition of its traditional super-power role while attempting to deal with economic weaknesses that stem from its lagging technology, continued reliance on energy exports, and the impact of economic sanctions.[16] Where other important players such as the G-20 and other advancing market economies fit in is determined by their own idiosyncratic mix of economic and political needs.

Stability or instability also will be determined by the strategies and political skills of national leaders. Leaders like Donald Trump and Xi Jinping play their hands aggressively, despite the great differences in their personalities, while weakened leaders like Emmanuel Macron, Angela Merkel, and British prime ministers David Cameron, Theresa May, and Boris Johnson faced different political realities.

Catastrophic events like pandemics, natural disasters, or other disruptive shocks to the system will make it more difficult to adjust to whatever level of transformation is occurring. Such challenges may overwhelm the attempts at "small fixes" and compel once cautious reformers to think about the now seemingly inevitable need for "big fixes." They may shift resources away from managing a relatively well-thought-out transformation of the economic and institutional order (at least in theory) and toward chaotic and uncertain crisis management. New economic and political wedge issues will emerge, both within and among nations, tempting nations and the politicians who lead them to seek opportunistic gain and place the blame for the disruption on "them," whoever they may be. Already weakened international economic institutions such as the WTO or regional trading blocs will be further compromised. What had begun as a reasonable and probably timely effort to "amend and reconfigure" the economic order turns into a disorderly and scrambled attempt to salvage what can be preserved, with each nation prioritizing its own needs ahead of the collective good.

What Would Globalization Amended and Reconfigured Look Like?

What would globalization amended and reconfigured look like? Disorderly, confused, and conflicted, much like today's world. It will be filled with institutions, treaties and multilateral agreements, and rules that tell us how the international economy should work. Some will continue to function, at least acceptably in most cases for most people, while others will be minimally effective, shunned, and at times ignored. It will also be filled with nations and leaders who demand change, in part because they believe the first phase of globalization has run its course and in part because they have found a useful political tool with which to win power. And while the call for "change" will be broadly heard, there will be great disagreement on what should be changed and how far the change should go. It will be an international system in transition, still overwhelmingly defined by economic realities but unsure of what comes next.

MERCANTILISM 2.0

Mercantilism 2.0 marks a significant shift in the paradigm. If fully implemented, it fundamentally changes the underlying rationale of why nations trade with one another. It's not the earlier notion that served as the justification for the empires of the past, and it's not the contemporary simplistic argument that can be summarized as just "economic nationalism" or "my country first" trade patterns. And it's not what we now call "developmental mercantilism," a temporary catch-up strategy for lagging nations to rapidly industrialize and graduate into the world of full-fledged members of the global economy. Rather, it attacks the fundamental arguments of Ricardo's theory of comparative advantage that say that economically motivated international trade is not a zero-sum game; everybody gains, although in the real world some benefit more than others. We have invented the "mercantilism 2.0" label to suggest that the revised doctrine is a new way to pursue a time-honored goal—the use of a nation's economic resources and foreign trade as a way to increase its power and influence in the international community.[17]

There are two elements, newly implemented in the context of the twenty-first century but historically consistent with the original version of mercantilism associated with Adam Smith's writings. First, it is about the *empowerment* of the nation-state, "the wealth of nations," as he put it.

It offers a full-throated and unapologetic defense of using national economic power as a legitimate foreign policy tool. The goal of national leaders is to advance the national interest, using all the tools at their disposal. That inevitably suggests movement away from a multilateral and rule-based trading regime, except when the nation-state in question decides that it's the best way to pursue its own national interest. But when it doesn't, other rules apply. . . .

That bring us to the second point about mercantilism 2.0: nation-states may sometimes decide not to play by the old playbook. It's not in their interest. Instead they become the major revisionist powers of the international order, going beyond "globalization amended and reconfigured" to demand more complete institutional and behavioral change. They become proactive agents of change, disruptive and sometimes destructive of the old order. Sometimes that takes the form of rewriting institutional structures (NAFTA to USMCA, or British abandonment of the EU). Sometimes it takes the form of unilaterally and creatively interpreting, or just breaking, the rules (Chinese industrial and currency exchange policies). And sometimes it takes the form of weaponizing elements of a nation's trade policy as leverage (the American use of tariffs "for reasons of national security," or boycotts and sanctions such as in its policy toward Russia, Syria, or Iran). The use of such "weapons" usually provokes a reaction. In the short-term, that may be limited to counter-sanctions and tariffs or to informal cooperation by other nations to create work-arounds and to isolate the offender. But in the long run, if the conflict deepens through round after round of tariffs, or if it spreads to other nations, more permanent institutional change, or perhaps the de-institutionalization of trade arrangements, may begin. A multilateral and rule-based system moves toward a series of multilateral or bilateral arrangements, with a slightly different set of rules for each engagement.

There is also another likely consequence, especially if the initial revisionist nations are successful: other nations will begin to apply their own versions of the same trade policies. There will be an international learning curve; If it works for America, or China, or Great Britain, or any of the other nations that are first to apply mercantilism 2.0, why won't it work for us? On the other hand, failure will also carry a message; if the early mercantilist 2.0 nations get little from their efforts, why go down the same road, or perhaps such a policy can work only for the economic superpowers but not for smaller nations?

What Is the Structure of Mercantilism 2.0?

At first, little is changed within the formal institutional structure of the existing arrangements. Nation-states, international institutions, and formalized trade regimes will continue to exist as they were, at least at first. The first hint of structural change will come when the initial mercantilist 2.0 nations begin to dissent from the existing order, to reinterpret the playbook and break the rules, and to demand changes because the system is not "fair" to them. There won't be many at first, but if their number includes major economic and military powers, they will have an impact. Perhaps they are emboldened to such action by larger changes in the international system; the Cold War ends, new superpowers emerge, and economic power shifts as globalization takes hold. Perhaps domestic politics brings new leaders to power; nations turn inward to deal with their own problems and grow tired of shouldering the responsibilities that made them world powers.

If their initiatives seem economically profitable and politically rewarding, then they will be tempted to deepen their commitment to change, and others will be tempted to follow. To force the revision of a regional trade pact like NAFTA in ways favorable to you or to win concessions from others through the real or threatened use of tariffs now seem like winning strategies. And to win election and reelection based on domestic support for such policies further confirms their popularity and tactical wisdom. It could produce the opposite result, of course. Aggressive trade policies could deepen and spread confrontation; what was once a trade dispute could fuel a more fundamental confrontation between economically and militarily powerful nations. Or perhaps it produces mixed results; it will work for some nations, but not for others. But most importantly, the game has been changed. There is a new chapter in the playbook, not quite yet proven, but tempting for anyone who wants to take the risk.

The rest of the world also will be changed as it tries to decide how to respond to mercantilism 2.0. The initial response will focus on condemnation of the disruption of the system. How can major economic powers like the United States or Great Britain back away from their post–World War II commitments to internationalism, collective security, and the Bretton Woods system, or from their responsibility to support the spread of liberal democracy, human rights, and international development? For the most part, they will not receive a satisfying answer, especially if other nations succumb to the my-country-first temptation. The initial responses will be "fixes" rather than "solutions," in part because it may just be a temporary aberration, a glitch caused by political instability, and it may cure itself. If it becomes apparent that it won't, the "fixes" turn to the renegotiation of existing arrangements. NAFTA becomes USMCA, or a series of bilateral trade deals operate alongside the multilateral agreements or WTO rules. Nations will negotiate ad hoc side agreements along with the formal trade pacts; if you don't impose a tariff, then we'll agree to admit more of your goods into our markets and buy a huge quantity of your soybeans or other agricultural products, and so on. Efforts to negotiate long-term institutional changes will be more difficult, especially if limited disputes turn into trade wars and stoke nationalist passions. The initial British effort to withdraw from the EU while preserving some degree of access to European markets quickly escalated into a major dispute that brought down two prime ministers (David Cameron and Theresa May) and eventually resulted in the landslide election of Boris Johnson, who secured the passage of a withdrawal agreement by an uncommonly compliant Tory majority in Commons.

The impact of mercantilism 2.0 on the G-7 and the G-20 will be mixed, and it will be increasingly difficult to find consensus within either about how to respond to the changing global economy. The inner core of the G-7 will maintain the greatest cohesion, with the United States remaining a wild card because of its political instability. The United

States undoubtedly will remain one of the strongest verbal proponents of mercantilism 2.0 policies, but pragmatism and internal political pressures will lead it to follow a more cautious path. Whatever the outcome of Brexit, Great Britain will exercise far less leadership. Within the EU, France and Germany will most likely remain the strongest supporters of some form of regional and global trade, supported by Canada and Japan. The continued commitment of Italy or other EU members prone to economic crises and political divisions over immigration is more questionable. The more diverse G-20 will be pulled in many different directions. China will set its own course, publicly supporting globalization while continuing to exploit its growing economic power through de facto mercantilist 2.0 policies and the growing reach of the Belt and Road projects. Japan, India, Indonesia, South Korea, South Africa, Argentina, Brazil, and Turkey will be torn between seeking a broader global role and securing their status as de facto regional powers. Mexico will be drawn even more closely into USMCA-based trade patterns. Russia, as always, will be a wildcard as a first-tier military power with a second-tier economy. It will likely fall back on its time-honored and usually successful strategy of playing the other G-7 and G-20 members against one another.

The world's reaction to mercantilism 2.0 will also be affected by its impact on broader geopolitical issues. The growing trade rivalries between the United States and China will stoke further military confrontation, especially for control of the western Pacific, and the disputed status of Taiwan will provide another potential flashpoint. While nowhere near a direct economic rival to the United States and China, Russia will provide another focal point of regional and global rivalries, especially if it forms a de facto alliance with China to isolate an increasingly disruptive United States. Further disruption is likely if emerging economic and military powers like India, Pakistan, Saudi Arabia, Iran, and Turkey also begin to employ a mercantilism 2.0 trade strategy, sharpening already existing disputes with their traditional rivals or provoking trade-based disagreements with once close trading partners.

More broadly, the potential spread of mercantilism 2.0 could have a profound impact on trading institutions. Pressures will mount to revise WTO rules, and disgruntled nations will threaten or actually initiate withdrawal proceedings. Some nations will find other ways to block WTO regulatory efforts. The United States has prevented the appointment of new judges to the panel that adjudicates trade disputes, making it impossible for the WTO to fulfill one of its most important functions. EU unity may be threatened by further "xits" or by breakaway new states like an independent Scotland or Catalonia seeking membership. NATO unity will be stressed by potentially new global realities, the risks of extending membership into central Europe, and the go-it-alone policies of key nations like the United States, as well as by disputes over strategy and cost sharing. Traditional trade regimes built around the Bretton Woods and WTO structures will be challenged by new formal institutions proffered as a "new" Bretton Woods and by seductive participation in China's Belt and Road arrangements and less formalized ad hoc ties.

The Distribution of Power in Mercantilism 2.0

As in a world of globalization amended and reconfigured, the first question is "the power to do what?" In mercantilism 2.0, the power to force change grows in proportion to the boldness of those nations that are willing to use it. "Power" in this case begins with the overall impact of nation's economy but must also include its willingness to take the political and economic risks of disrupting the system and accepting the short-term economic hardships and countermeasures that will occur. It's not for the faint of heart or for a second- or third-tier nation with limited economic impact, except perhaps on a regional basis. If the initiators are successful in bringing change, a domino effect begins to take place. A few nations initiate the challenge to the conventional and institutionalized practices. A maturing developmental neomercantilist nation like China presses its advantage and refuses to "graduate," and others follow suit. Unquestionably, mature industrial economies like Japan or South Korea practice some degree of protectionism, restricting foreign access to their markets.

Other nations demand institutional changes, some subtle, such as a selective redefinition of existing trade regimes or multilateral agreements, and some not so subtle, such as withdrawal from the EU or USMCA. Some, like the United States, launch a series of attacks on the existing global and regional arrangements, initially demanding extensive change but eventually settling for more modest outcomes. The success of one or more of the initial revisionists emboldens others. More dominos fall until the revisions have run their course, and a new set of institutions and a new playbook have emerged.

Viewed from a broader perspective, it becomes a selective policy of coercive transactionalism based on the application of a nation's economic power to obtain both economic and broader political goals. It is coercive in the same sense that coercive diplomacy, long accepted as a tool of a nation's foreign policy, seeks to influence another nation through the application of a set of economic sanctions and rewards, most often on a country-by-country basis. America's threat to withdraw from NAFTA unless fundamental changes occurred ultimately resulted in a series of separate bilateral talks with Mexico and Canada that produced the USMCA, an amended and modestly reconfigured version of the old regional trade agreement. The important point from our perspective is how the new agreement was reached. The United States employed its dominant economic power first to disrupt the old institutional order and then to separately negotiate its replacement on a bilateral basis in which it could play Mexico and Canada against each other.

Power to protect the existing global and regional trade arrangements is quite another thing. On the one hand, it is likely well institutionalized and sustained by the inertia of post–World War II practices. It's conventional wisdom, and for most but not all, a comfort zone meaning prosperity and international acceptance. It will have many defenders: the first-tier industrial nations that have not experienced wide-scale social or economic disruption from globalization; the second-tier industrialized nations that have found a solid but not dominant niche in global supply chains; and the emerging industrial and market economies that have struggled to join a global economy that has been their role model for decades.

But on the other hand, institutionalization and business-as-usual inertia will do little to deter nations that seek fundamental change. For those nations, many of which initially led the creation of free trade regimes and the global economy in the 1970s and 1980s, globalization may have reached a point of diminishing returns. They have nothing more to gain from it, and the growing social and political costs now exceed any future marginal returns. It's run its course, and maybe gone too far, and now it's time to reassess the balance. Other elements of the changing international system strengthen the backlash. As chapter 2 points out, the resurgence of the nation-state as a key player strengthens the perception that national economic well-being should be prioritized. And as chapters 3 and 4 will add, the rediscovery of a unique cultural identity or ideology strengthens the argument. Politics will play a role as well. The purely economic argument aside, mercantilism 2.0 is a powerful political force in an uncertain world and in once-dominant nations that fear that their best days may be behind them. It wins elections, at least sometimes, and that will lure hopeful candidates and frustrated voters to its banner.

Sources of Stability and Instability in Mercantilism 2.0

"Stability" is a relative term in the world of mercantilism 2.0. Like globalization amended and reconfigured, mercantilism 2.0 is a work in progress. Things are changing, but we aren't sure how much. Mercantilism 2.0 may be too disruptive, leading even its original proponents to take a step back and accept an amended and reconfigured version of globalization. But on the other hand, change may accelerate out of control, producing the world of "autarky and anarchy," as the next section describes it. On the side of instability is the temptation for other nations to turn to mercantilism 2.0, in part because it seems to work for some nations and in part because of its appeal to the voters. On the side of stability are the institutionalized trade regimes, the fact that the vast majority of nations want order and predictability in their trading relationships, and the probable reality that even the strongest nations that initiated mercantilism 2.0 eventually want things to settle down, albeit in a way more advantageous to them.

Disruptive events like pandemics, natural disasters, or manmade shocks to the system resulting from wars or migrations will further deepen the propensity of individual nation-states to go their own way. It will all depend on the nature of the crisis and, perhaps more importantly, how it is interpreted by political leaders. If its impact is widespread, transcending national and regional borders, there may be some attempt to rebuild the now diminished mechanisms of a multilateral response. But if it is defined primarily in national terms, as a sort of zero-sum game in which each nation completes for resources or casts blame on others as the cause of the problem, it will strengthen the politically tempting tendency to pit "us" against "them" and seek responses at the national level. The economically and politically more powerful nations will have the edge in opting out of coordinated action, while the poorer and less powerful nations will be at the mercy of the of the lowest common denominator that the international system can provide in the face of growing division.

What Would a Mercantilism 2.0 World Look Like?

A new equilibrium—or *equilibriums*—could emerge. The singular version takes us back to a more radically altered "amended and reconfigured" world in which a new normal emerges that almost everybody accepts, perhaps grudgingly, for the sake of moving on. Perhaps we should call it "compulsory globalization 2.0," familiar and mutually profitable, but different. What remains of global trade will operate at the pleasure of the dominant economic powers, subject to their periodic unilateral revision. Both the formal institutions and the informal playbook have been restructured and rewritten by the dominant powers. Most of the time, the modus operandi will be clear and predictable to all trading nations, large and small. The system will inherently favor the more powerful trading nations, particularly those that initially disrupted the old order. But for the most part, all major trading nations will accept the new rules of the game and the nature of the new playing field. In short, things will settle down into a new business-as-usual sort of way.

The plural version—*equilibriums*—is more complex. In reality there are two "systems," the first based on a partially successful recrafting of the old order; a form of globalization survives, amended and reconfigured, structuring international trade for most nations most of the time. But there is a second parallel alternative reality in which the major economic powers *may, if they choose*, play by different rules when it suits their purpose, working through coercive transactionalism to create new bilateral trade arrangements, imposing tariffs or sanctions, or linking trade policy to other noneconomic issues. In some ways, it is analogous to the veto power given to the five permanent members of the United Nations Security Council. Most of the time, and on most of the issues that do not affect their core interests, the permanent members refrain from using their veto, informally seeking compromises through negotiation or, in rare cases, abstaining from the formal vote. Only when an issue is considered to be vitally important do they cast a formal veto, admittedly some far more frequently than others. Unlike the formalized UN veto power, the de facto power granted to dominant economic powers is an informal arrangement, the best that could be reached under the circumstances. It's somewhere between a formally amended and reconfigured globalist system and a continuing downward spiral into autarky and anarchy. It's a compromise, political more than economic, that accepts the unfair but underlying reality of the international system: all nations are not equally powerful, and sometimes they play by different rules. Most of the time, the major economic powers will accept the day-to-day operational code and make the best of it. But there will be times that they exercise their "special" prerogative not to play by the rules. As with the Security Council veto, over time other nations will learn to predict when that is likely to occur and how to deal with it.

Toward Autarky, with a Touch of Anarchy

"Toward autarky" does not mean complete autarky (which means complete self-sufficiency) which is impossible in the modern world. But rather toward a world in which coercive aggressive mercantilism 2.0 and coercive transactionalism have become the new normal of economic exchanges. It's a familiar but not completely predictable world, but the stakes are higher. Once the policies of choice for major nations that decided to weaponize their economic power for national advantage, or for declining powers that sought to preserve some semblance of control, mercantilism 2.0 and coercive transactionalism have broadened and deepened. *Broadening* means that more nations adopted it as a major component of their trade policy, perhaps because it seemed to work in the hands of another nation, and perhaps because it was politically popular at home. *Deepening* means that it has spread to all sectors of the national economies involved, designed to protect more than a few at-risk activities such as agriculture or selected domestic industries. Now it is the weapon of first choice, and everything is a part of a policy to buy, eat, drink, drive, watch, or listen to domestically produced products. What had been a global economy fractures into a network of smaller blocs and ad hoc trading regimes. Some are still viable, if much diminished in terms of productive capacity and consumption. Others fare less well, spiraling downward into economic isolation and hardship, and perhaps eventual social and political instability.

The results will be mixed. For the major economies, and for those nations like the United States, China, and Great Britain that led the way in the mercantilism 2.0 revolution, the outcome will be mitigated by their inherent advantages: existing, if perhaps dated, industrial stock, technology, labor resources, and a large internal market. They will prosper in a world moving toward greater autarky, diminished but not broken, especially if we remember that "prosper" will be a relative term. Large regional trading blocs like the EU also are well positioned to adapt to the new reality, especially if they develop trade ties with China and Belt and Road nations and manage their own inherent political tensions. Russia will slowly decline in terms of economic and military power, perhaps sustained by continued energy exports and closer economic ties with China's Belt and Road network. The prosperity of key European nations will depend on the economic viability and political cohesion of the EU. Great Britain, or potentially what's left of it after Brexit and possible Scottish independence and the unification of Northern Ireland and the Republic of Ireland, will face hard times, despite efforts to evoke its "special relationship" with the United States and the Commonwealth nations. Whatever the specific geographic outcome, overall trade patterns will shift toward ad hoc bilateral and more limited multilateral agreements, and regional trade blocs will become more important as an opportunity for emerging regional hegemons to assert their influence or for smaller countries to seek safe haven in difficult times.

The Structure of an Increasingly Autarkic World

The growing power of economically prosperous nation-states, especially those that spearheaded mercantilism 2.0 and now more widely practice coercive transactionalism, will be the most significant structural feature of an increasingly autarkic world. It will be an increasingly pre–Bretton Woods and pre-globalization arrangement, more hierarchical and conflicted. Competition among nation-states will intensify, both to protect economic resources needed for autarky and to preserve those still-surviving trade relationships that remain essential. The world will once again play a series of zero-sum games, and the memory of win-win scenarios will recede into the past. While the institutionalized trade regimes such as the WTO or regional arrangements like the EU will continue to function, especially for nations or blocs unable to sustain themselves in greater isolation, they will hold sway over a diminishing volume of international commerce. Trade and tariff wars will become commonplace, pitting the stronger surviving economies against one another and increasing their ability to dictate terms to second- and third-tier economies. Global supply chains will atrophy, replaced with more regionalized or entirely indigenous counterparts. Multilateral corporations will be under strong pressure to cut international ties and repatriate production facilities, technology, and capital to the homeland.

Increasing autarky will also have broader political impact on multilateral institutions. The United Nations and the major regional groupings such as the Organization of American States will be less able to undertake peacemaking or peacekeeping efforts. "Responsibility to protect" (R2P) humanitarian programs to deal with human rights violations, genocide, medical emergencies, or famine also will be diminished, as will other multilateral efforts to deal with environmental deterioration, global warming, or pandemics, to name but a few.

Nations will be faced with difficult choices that define their place in an increasingly autarkic world. What can we produce on our own? Can domestic production meet the needs of our people? What can we export in an increasingly autarkic world, and can it support our need to import those things that we cannot produce on our own? In a worst-case scenario, what can we live without, and what are the social and political costs of such decisions? Who will pay the costs or reap the benefits of such shrinkage? While a few nations will contemplate complete economic isolationism similar to North Korea's policy of *juche* (self-reliance), most will face serious and destabilizing trade-offs.

Another old question will arise, last heard at Bretton Woods: To what extent should the relatively successful nations encourage at least a modicum of economic stability and prosperity in other nations as a way of forestalling future wars? With economic hardship expanding and the memories of two world wars and the Cold War fading, willingness to take on such efforts may be difficult to muster.

How Is Power Distributed in an Autarkic World?

Power is more concentrated into the hands of those nations that best adapt to increasing autarky. It will be an increasingly hierarchical world, and high position in the pecking order will convey greater power to control others and less responsibility to work for the common good. Not surprisingly the United States and China will head the list, the first because of its inherent advantages in size, diversity, resources, and domestic market, and the latter because it possesses similar advantages, enhanced by the proactive industrial and trade policy of its government. Moreover, the United States will dominate the USMCA, and China will have growing influence in the Belt and Road nations reaching from Asia to Europe. The EU will remain a major trade bloc and avoid the worst excesses of autarky, although internal economic and political squabbles between France and Germany and periodic crises in Italy, Greece, or Spain will take their toll. Russia will remain a major military power, weakened by its lagging technology, weak foreign direct investment, and reliance on energy exports. The bottom half of the G-20 will languish, and aspiring nations now further down the pecking order will find it difficult to move up. Developmental neomercantilism will cease to be effective as a growth strategy in a world in which export-driven economies will find few foreign markets for their goods.

The power of the multilateral institutions such as the WTO and the other remnants of the Bretton Woods system will atrophy. As nations adopt "my country first" priorities implemented through coercive transactionalism, they will turn to such bodies only if they are powerful enough to exploit them to their own ends or so weak that they have no other alternative but to seek collective action. Either way, institutions of a once globalized world will be a pale reflection of their former selves.

Some semblance of a multinational order may survive from the possible continuing viability of regional trading blocs. Three things will be required: First, the economic viability of the bloc will be based on internally sustainable trading patterns, including possession of or access to raw materials and energy, sufficiently advanced technology and a well trained workforce, and a sufficiently large market within the bloc to sustain consumption. Second, the bloc must be able and willing to work out whatever political issues may arise between its members, and the bloc's leading members must be internally politically stable. And third, conflict between competing blocs must be kept at a minimum through diplomacy and/ or deterrence, perhaps permitting limited bloc-to-bloc trade. It won't be the beginning of a new move toward globalization, but it will perhaps be sufficient to provide a modicum of economically rational and politically acceptable international trade.

Sources of Stability and Instability

In the short term, stability in an increasingly autarkic world may depend in part on the lowering of expectations about what is now possible and on how fragile the new arrangements really are. With globalization now in full retreat, nothing remains to inspire nation-states beyond their own self-interest. A new international system has been created, and now we'll have to live with its successes and shortcomings. The viability of regional trading blocs will offer some sense of order and stability, especially if bloc members accept the de facto dominance of its leading member (probably easier in a U.S.-dominated USMCA and a Chinese-dominated Belt and Road bloc, less so in the EU because of long-standing German-French competition), and if the blocs work out some sense of post-globalist peaceful coexistence. Eventually, there will be some effort to cobble together a new Bretton Woods system, perhaps built on the success of internal governance and stabilization efforts initially undertaken within the blocs themselves, but it will be a slow and halting process.

The failure of the once-successful Bretton Woods system may eventually become a strong motivation to revisit the creation of multilateral institutions. While some nations and blocs will prosper, others will merely survive, or worse. It is likely that failed and rogue nations will emerge in the sharpened rivalries of a post-globalist world, and that their difficulties will disrupt whatever is left of international order. If the memory of the post-1929 depression and World War II were sufficient to inspire the creators of the Bretton Woods system and a global economy, then the fallout of post-globalism hardships and conflicts may reanimate their broader concerns at some point in the future.

The sources of instability in an autarkic world are many. Regional trading blocs may atrophy, and new ones fail to form. Or they may stoke bloc-to-bloc rivalries, at first probably economic but eventually geopolitical and military in their implications. Key member nations within a bloc may succumb to internal instability, or bloc members may revive old conflicts among themselves. Normal market fluctuations and periodic crises will have greater impact. A growth strategy based on developmental neo-mercantilism and an export-driven economy is now less viable, leaving many once hopeful nations languishing or falling behind. The distance between *have* and *have-not* nations and regions will widen. Nations that once accepted the validity of a developmental model that assured their eventual full-fledged membership in a global economy may now turn inward, evoking extreme forms of nationalism or seeking distinct cultural or ideological answers to their problems.

Catastrophic events like natural disasters, pandemics, and the myriad impacts of civil and international wars, to say nothing of failed states, will confirm the existence of an autarkic and every-nation-for-itself world. Overall system capabilities to deal with common problems will be seriously eroded, and the political will to rebuild even a nascent multilateral system will be absent, at least until the costs of continued disunion become unbearable. It will be a very fragile world and risky for all but the most power nation-states that survive, albeit in diminished form. Given the political and institutional terrain of the new order, even powerful nations will be more inclined to respond defensively to most challenges, seeing little short-term advantage to be gained from a more proactive long-term response to solve multinational problems rather than just managing their immediate impact on the home nation. Unanticipated and unmanaged shocks to the system can only complicate such a fragile international order, further driving autarky toward anarchy.

What Would a World of Autarky, with a Touch of Anarchy, Look Like?

A world of autarky, with a touch of anarchy, would be a world characterized by a much higher level of economic and political instability, which would be mutually reinforcing. It would live on the edge of multiple potential crises linked to market volatility, political instability, and increasing competition among the major economic powers and their newly constituted blocs. At best, it could maintain an unstable balance between the forces of stability and instability constantly pulling it in different directions, one toward further enhancement of economic nationalism and the unilateral power of the dominant nations, the other toward the deepening of a new and far less robust commitment multilateral institutions—a mini–Bretton Woods system, or something like it—that would try to provide a greater sense of order and predictability. It would be an exciting, volatile, and dangerous world in which to live.

NOTES

1. Peter N. Stearns, *The Industrial Revolution in World History* (Routledge, 2012); Klaus Schwab, *The Fourth Industrial Revolution* (Currency, 2017); Jeremy Rifkin, *The Third Industrial Revolution* (St. Martin's Griffin, 2013).

2. Adam Smith, *The Wealth of Nations* (Cedar Lakes Classics, 2019, first published in 1776); J. W. Horrocks, *A Short History of Mercantilism* (Routledge, 2018); and Philip J. Stern and Carl Wennerlind, eds., *Mercantilism Reimagined: Political Economy in Early Modern Britain and Its Empire* (Oxford University Press, 2013).

3. David Ricardo, *The Principles of Political Economy and Taxation* (Dover, 2004, first published in 1817); Kimberly Clausing, *Open: The Progressive Case for Free Trade, Immigration, and Global Capital* (Harvard University Press, 2019); Douglas Irwin, *Free Trade under Fire*, 4th ed. (Princeton University Press, 2015); and Ralph Folsom, *Free Trade Agreements: From GATT 1947 to NAFTA Renegotiated 2018* (West Academic Publishing, 2019).

4. Peter Lichtenstein, *Theories of International Economics* (Routledge, 2016), 12–33; and Peter Pham, "Why Do All Roads Lead to China?" *Forbes*, March 20, 2018.

5. Manfreid B. Steger, *Globalization: A Very Short Introduction* (Oxford University Press, 2017); Joseph E. Stiglitz, *Globalization and Its Discontents* (Norton, 2017); and Dani Rodrik, *The Globalization Paradox: Democracy and the Future of the World Economy* (Norton, 2012).

6. Benn Steil, *The Battle of Bretton Woods: John Maynard Keyes, Harry Dexter White, and the Making of a New World Order* (Princeton University Press, 2014); Ed Conway, *The Summit: Bretton Woods 1944* (Pegasus, 2016); Eric Helleiner, *The Forgotten Foundation of Bretton Woods, International Development and the Making of the Postwar Order* (Cornell University Press, 2016); Frederick S. Weaver, *The United States and the Global Economy: From Bretton Woods to the Current Crisis* (Rowman & Littlefield, 2011); Bernard M. Hoekman, *World Trade Organization (WTO): Law, Economics, and Politics*, 2nd ed. (Routledge, 2015); Ngaire Woods, *The Globalizers: The IMF, the World Bank, and Their Borrowers* (Cornell University Press, 2007); Katherine Marshall, *The World Bank: From Reconstruction to Development to Equity* (Routledge, 2007); Mark S. Coplovitch, *The International Monetary Fund in the Global Economy: Banks, Bonds, and Bailouts*

(Cambridge University Press, 2010); and James Raymond Vreeland, *The International Monetary Fund: The Politics of Conditional Lending* (Routledge, 2006).

7. Ian Nederveen Pieterse, *Globalization and Culture: Global Melange* (RI, 2015); and John Tomlinson, *Globalization and Culture* (University of Chicago Press, 1999).

8. Barry Eichengreen, *The European Economy since 1945: Coordinated Capitalism and Beyond* (Princeton University Press, 2008); Mark Gilbert, *European Integration: A Concise History*, rev. ed. (Rowman & Littlefield, 2011); Andrew Duff, ed., *Maastricht and Beyond* (Routledge, 1994); Desmond Dinan, *Europe Recast: A History of the European Union*, 2nd ed. (Lynne Rienner, 2014); Mikhail J. Boskin, ed., *NAFTA at 20: The North American Trade Agreement and Challenges* (Hoover Institution Press, 2014); David A. Lynch, *Trade and Globalization: An Introduction to Regional Trade Agreements* (Rowman & Littlefield, 2010); Robert Looney, *Handbook of International Trade Agreements: Country, Regional, and Global Approaches* (Routledge, 2018); and World Trade Organization, *Regional Trade Agreements and the Multilateral Trading System*, (World Trade Organization, 2016).

9. World Bank, *Global Economic Prospects: Broad-Based Upturn, but For How Long?* (World Bank, 2018); World Bank, *Global Economic Prospects: Darkening Skies* (World Bank, 2019); Paul Krugman, *The Return of Depression Economics and the Crisis of 2008* (Norton, 2008); Ben S. Bernanke, Timothy F. Geithner, and Henry M. Paulson Jr., *Firefighting: The Financial Crisis and Its Lessons* (Penguin, 2009); and Carmen M. Reinhardt and Kenneth S. Rogoff, *This Time It's Different: Eight Centuries of Financial Folly* (Princeton University Press, 2011).

10. Ivo H. Daalder and James M. Lindsay, *The Empty Throne: America's Abdication of Global Leadership* (Public Affairs, 2018); Richard Haass, *A World in Disarray: American Foreign Policy and the Crisis of the Old Order* (Penguin, 2018); Joseph S. Nye, *Is the American Century Over?* (Polity, 2015); Hal Brands, *American Grand Strategy in the Age of Trump* (Brookings Institution, 2018); and Pippa Norris, *Cultural Backlash: Trump, Brexit, and Authoritarian Populism* (Cambridge University Press, 2019).

11. Nigel Culkin, *Tales of Brexits Past and Present: Understanding the Choices, Threats, and Opportunities* (Emerald Publishers, 2018); Harold D. Clarke and Matthew Goodwin Whiteley, *Why Britain Voted to Leave the European Union* (Cambridge University Press, 2017); and Geoffrey Evans and Anand Menon, *Brexit and British Politics* (Polity, 2017).

12. Congressional Research Service, *China-U.S. Trade Issues* (Congressional Research Service, 2019); Julien Chaisse, ed., *China's International Investment Strategy: Bilateral, Regional, and Global: Law and Policy* (Oxford University Press, 2019); Shuxiu Zhang, *Chinese Economic Diplomacy* (Routledge, 2016); Barry J. Naughten, *The Chinese Economy: Adaptation and Growth* (MIT Press, 2018); June Grasso, Jay P. Corrin, and Michael Kort, *Modernization and Revolution in China*, 5th ed. (Routledge, 2017); Peter Navarro and Greg Autry, *Death by China* (Pearson, 2011); John Bryan Starr, *Understanding China: A Guide to China's Economy, History, and Political Culture* (Hill and Wang, 2010); and Peter Frankopan, *The New Silk Road: The Present and the Future of the World* (Knopf, 2019).

13. John W. Dower, *Embracing Defeat: Japan in the Wake of World War II* (Norton, 2000); Frances McCall Rosenbluth, *Japan Transformed: Political Change and Economic Restructuring* (Princeton University Press, 2010); Koichi Namada, ed., *Japan's Bubble, Deflation,*

and Long-term Stagnation (MIT Press, 2010); Masazumi Wakatabe, *Japan's Great Stagnation and Abenomics* (Palgrave Macmillan, 2015).

14. Jonathan Olsen and John McCormick, *The European Union: Politics and Policies* (Westview, 2016); Catherine E. DeVries, *Euroscepticism and the Future of European Integration* (Oxford University Press, 2018); Simon Bulmer, *Germany and the European Union: Europe's Reluctant Hegemon?* (Red Globe, 2018); and Manuel Castells et al., *Europe's Crisis* (Polity, 2018).

15. Richard J. Barnett and Ronald E. Muller, *Global Reach: The Power of Multinational Corporations* (Touchstone, 1976); and Alfred D. Chandler, *Leviathans: Multinational Corporations and the New Global History* (Cambridge University Press, 2005).

16. Donald R. Kelley, *Russian Politics and Presidential Power: Transformational Leadership from Gorbachev to Putin* (CQ/SAGE, 2017); Richard Sakwa, *Russia's Futures* (Polity, 2019); Fiona Hill and Clifford G. Gaddy, *Mr. Putin: Operative in the Kremlin* (Brookings Institution, 2015); Angela Stent, *Putin's World: Russia Against the West and with the Rest* (Twelve Publishers, 2019); and Michael McFaul, *From Cold War to Hot Peace* (Houghton Mifflin Harcourt, 2019).

17. John B. Judis, *The Nationalist Revival: Trade, Immigration, and the Revolt against Globalization* (Columbia Global Reports, 2018); John B. Judis, *The Populist Explosion: How the Great Recession Transformed American and European Politics* (Columbia Global Reports, 2016); Roger Eatwell, *National Populism: The Revolt against Liberal Democracy* (Penguin Random House, 2018); and Eric Helleiner and Andreas Pickel, *Economic Nationalism in a Globalizing World* (Cornell University Press, 2004).

4

The Identity and Culture Paradigm

THE PARADIGM

Identity and culture become increasingly important in defining the international system, reshaping domestic politics within nation-states and redefining the issues and fault lines of international politics. While the nation-state and economic factors remain significant parts of how we interact, they are increasingly viewed through our own cultural prism. Who we are, both as individuals and cultures, shapes our perception of the nation-state within which we live and our position in the broader international system. The important question is how we use these identities as guidelines to action.[1]

What Do We Mean by Identity and Culture?

Each of us has many different identities. We have a *personal identity* that tells us who we are as individuals. But we also have a *collective identity* that includes a broader sense of who we are in terms of the culture within which we live. The two interact, probably differently for each of us, to produce an overall picture of who we are (the individual identity) and how we fit into the broader world around us (the collective identity). Both also tell us who we aren't, producing what psychologists call the *other*, sorting out the world in terms of *in-groups* (those who are like us) and *out-groups* (those who aren't like us). How seriously we take those distinctions becomes the foundation of an international system based on identity and culture.

Our personal identity tells us who we are and where we fit in, and some part of it is critically important to determining our political identity. It is an artificially crafted self-image we invent for ourselves, partly made up of our own unique self-image but mostly composed of things we borrow from the world around us. It includes a lot of things: gender, age (usually in terms of generational identity), sexual orientation, race, nationality, ethnicity, religion, language, occupation, lifestyle, urban or rural residence, family history, philosophical orientation, political or partisan identity, and whatever else we think makes us, well, us. Most of those markers are not particular to us alone. They come from the broader social context within which we live, and give us reference points in constructing our identity. You cannot decide that you are French, for example, until you learn that there is a larger reality out there called France with which you can identify. And like many reference points, the notion of being French carries with it a lot of other things: a national homeland, language, history, culture, religion, and more. The same would be true for most other nationalities such as German, or Russian, or Japanese. But what if the reference points were less clear or internally conflicted? What if you identify as an American, that is, a citizen of the United States of America, or as British, a citizen of the United Kingdom of Great Britain and Northern Ireland? Both are more complex political entities containing within them far greater diversity in terms of potential identity choices. You would probably still work it out in terms of creating your own personal identity, but the task would be more complex, forcing you to make difficult choices.

The same is true of all of the other elements of our identity. Some seem objectively determined and open to little doubt: if you were born into a family that has lived in France for generations, you are probably going to grow up accepting most of the "package" that constitutes French identity. But what if you are of mixed heritage; your father was French and your mother was American? And then you went to Oxford University in

Great Britain? And married a Chinese girl you met there, whose father was a high-ranking government official in Beijing? Or what if you were a first-generation immigrant from a former French colony? Or a political refugee from the turmoil of the Middle East? Or, for whatever personal reason, you simply reject the culture into which you were born? It could go on and on, but you probably get the point by now: in the modern world, personal identities are likely to be increasingly complex and internally conflicted.

What is our *collective identity*, and what does it tell us? Like our personal identity, it is a social construct and cognitive framework that sets the stage around us. We pretty much take it for granted. It answers most of the questions we ask on a day-to-day basis and provides a comfort zone within which we function. At times, of course, it may not be so reassuring: we are changing, or the broader culture around us is changing, causing us to question old truths. Or we have discovered a *latent identity*, something about us that never seemed important until now, like religion, ethnicity, social class, or occupation, that forces us to reexamine an identity that no longer seems adequate.

For our purposes, that broader sense of collective identity is generally called *culture* or, more broadly, *civilization*. The dictionary calls it "the customs, beliefs, social forms, and material traits of a racial, religious, or social group."[2] It is our collective identity writ large, the big picture. For most of us, it is the ultimate reference point that defines us, and the menu from which we choose when we construct our own personal identity. Most of the time, we do not consciously think about it, either because we take it as a given or because it seems secure and everlasting. But at other times, its importance to us may be overwhelming. Perhaps the culture is changing, and we are fearful that our sense of identity is in danger. Or perhaps it is not changing fast enough; society is changing more rapidly than the culture, which seems out-of-date and mired in the past. More disturbingly, perhaps *we* (meaning our culture or civilization) are in conflict with *them* (another culture or civilization) in what we perceive to be a life-or-death struggle.

From Culture to Civilization

Attention to the role of cultural identity as a driving force in the post–Cold War world significantly increased with the publication of Samuel P. Huntington's *The Clash of Civilizations and the Remaking of the World Order* in 1996.[3] This seminal but deeply controversial work enlarged the frame of reference from *cultures* to *civilizations*, which Huntington described as "the ultimate human tribes, and the clash of civilizations is tribal conflict on a global scale." With the Cold War behind us, analysts groped for a new frame of reference to describe the new world order. Some saw it as American hegemony, at least for a while, while others viewed it as the reemergence of a multipolar world. Yet others envisioned an increasingly globalized world regulated by international and multinational institutions like the European Union, a strengthened United Nations, or new rule-based institutions like the World Trade Organization. Francis Fukuyama, who had served on the Policy Planning staff of the U.S. Department of State, spoke of an even more radical transformation in his 1992 book *The End of History and the Last Man*, which argued that the world of old-fashioned geopolitics and the balance of power created by the Westphalian system were forever gone.[4] He was less enlightening about what would follow, except to argue that "history" had finished the game of geopolitics and would now be shaped by the universalization of Western liberal democracy as the final form of human government.

Huntington was far less optimistic, arguing that the future fault lines of international conflict would be based on differences among civilizations writ large. He divided the post–Cold War world into eight civilizations, some more clearly articulated than others: Sinic (Chinese), Japanese, Hindu, Islamic, Orthodox, Latin American, African, and Western, all discussed at great length below.

In the post–Cold War world, the most significant fault lines would be defined by disputes both within and among these civilizations, with victory or defeat measured not just in terms of military strength or economic power but also in terms of the supposed superiority of the underlying culture. Such confrontations would take one of two configurations: 1) along the fault lines at which different cultures come into contact (for example, the geographic boundaries separating Catholic Western Europe and Orthodox Eastern Europe, although some countries such as Ukraine or Bosnia Herzegovina would be internally divided), or 2) between the "core" states of different cultures (for example, long-standing hostilities between Russia and China or between the United States and China or Japan).

The identity and culture paradigm posits:

- **Identity and culture will increasingly play the dominant role in shaping the international system.**

At the individual level, identity and culture reshape the perception of self in ways that emphasize elements that identify with cultural reference points. "I am a . . . ," and what comes next goes beyond the legalistic definition of formal citizenship to a more deeply rooted sense of being a part of a larger cultural identity. To be sure, the distinctions between cultural identity and other markers are never precise. A sense of national identity frequently overlaps with a sense of cultural identity, especially if the nation-state in question is what Huntington calls the "core" of a civilization. At that individual level, it is a recognition and deeply meaningful reaffirmation of one's "roots," a back-to-the-future feeling that our future depends on understanding our past. Openly or implicitly, it argues that something has been "lost"—a sense of values, or unity, or destiny—that must be rediscovered.

At the collective level, identity usually is manifested in one of three ways. First and most commonly, it emerges through the traditional notion of nationalism, a fusion of geography (we have our own nation-state, the Westphalian culmination of any people's quest) and culture (we are a like-minded and coherent community, with a common culture containing many overlapping identity markers such as language, history, religion, and whatever else seems important to us). The sense of unity and common identity is stronger if the nation-state is the core state of a larger civilization. A modified sense of common national and cultural identity can also be present in diaspora communities, especially if they maintain unity within the host nation and close ties to the core community.

Second, a sense of continuing collective identity can be based on the presence of common attributes that do not necessarily include identification with or aspirations to create a core state. A common religion and culture may be sufficient, especially if the community chooses not to be well integrated into the host nation or is the target of discrimination or rejection. For example, émigré refugee communities may attempt to maintain some degree of isolation to preserve their culture and sense of community, as with Muslim settlement in the Molenbeek district in Brussels or, on a long-term basis, the Parsi community in India.

Third, and less frequently, a community may sustain its collective identity through a sense of a common destiny or fate, most often tied to an evangelical religious, cultural, or political movement, as with efforts to restore a Muslim caliphate in the Middle East. The other side of the coin also applies: a common identity can be the product of perceived victimization in which the primary definition of *us* lies in what *they* have done to *us*, as with the Jewish diaspora community before the creation of Israel.

- **Identity- and culture-based conflict is more absolutist, involving distinctions between *us* and *them*, making it far more difficult to find common ground or to mediate disputes.**

Disputes rooted in conflicting identities and cultures are far more abstract and intangible than geopolitical or economic disputes. They are about in-group and out-group distinctions and a sense of tribal loyalty. At stake are the affirmation and validation of core values that are deeply rooted in both self- and collective identities. It is about religion, race, truth, the validity of our past, and our hopes for the future—all of those things that engender deep emotional as well as intellectual commitment. And it is *our* truth, most likely the only real truth in a world of false prophets. We have a commitment to defend it to the death, and perhaps to bring it to others who are misled and unenlightened. We are called to become its missionaries, and perhaps its missionary warriors, and our victory will affirm the superiority and correctness of our culture.

Such commitment makes it difficult to resolve disputes. Old-fashioned geopolitical disputes (where the border between our two countries ought to be) can be resolved by negotiations, and economic disputes (what should be the terms of our next trade agreement) are subject to the art of the deal, at least in theory. But disputes over truth, destiny, and fealty to the tribe and the faith are not easily compromised by splitting the difference and moving on. To be sure, there are ways to try to deal with such disputes. Conventional diplomacy, mediation, arbitration, or the use of international courts are all helpful, especially if the opposing parties all accept the same playbook and are motivated to resolve the issue peacefully. More complicated arrangements are sometimes helpful, at least in the short run. Power-sharing arrangements are one option. Lebanon had brief success with a form of government called "consociationalism," in which power is shared among ethnic and/or religious factions, while other similar efforts in Cyprus, Bosnia and Herzegovina, and Northern Ireland have enjoyed mixed results at best. Formal separation is another possibility, as with the division of Ireland into the sovereign Republic of Ireland and Northern Ireland, which remains a part of the United Kingdom. At the individual-identity level, the acceptance of a "hyphenated identity" is another response, as long as the various *something-Americans* or other hyphenated citizens can handle the dualism and ambiguity. Identity substitution, or displacement, is commonly attempted to forge new individual and collective identities. It lay at the core of the Treaty of Westphalia's creation of "new" national identities, and it is commonly associated with profound social revolutions (France's efforts after revolution to create a secular French identity, and similar efforts at social engineering after the Russian, Turkish, and Chinese revolutions). It has enjoyed mixed success at best, especially over the long timeframe; sometimes it works, at least for a while, but the roots of the original identity are deep.

- **The identity and culture paradigm conceptualizes the future in terms of the growing significance of individual and collective social identities and the importance of cultural fault lines**

rather than geopolitical or economic factors in determining the structure and modus operandi of the international system.

In practical terms, this does not mean that the long list of formal actors such as the nation-state or international and multinational bodies like the United Nations will disappear. It does suggest that the actions of their members will be increasingly guided by each nation's sense of identity. For the conventional nation-state, this means that a sense of national identity will be increasingly linked to a perception of common cultural identity rather than to emphasis on the more legalistic sense of *citizenship* per se. For sprawling multicultural nations like the United States or Russia, the discovery of a common cultural heritage may be difficult and lead to bitter and disruptive battles over who the "real" Americans or Russians are, to be sorted out in terms of "when you got there" and the other conflict-prone markers such as race, ethnicity, language, religion, national origin, or whatever else divides us. It will not be easy or peaceful, and it will fuel deep and divisive political battles. Nations like Great Britain that had been pieced together over the years through a series of agreements such as the Acts of Union in 1707, which joined England and Scotland, will likely find their continued unity sorely tested. Other more culturally homogeneous nations like Hungary or Poland or those, like France, that historically promoted the assimilation of new peoples and cultures will find the transition less disruptive.

Predicting how the increasing salience of cultural identity will affect the interaction *among* nations is far more difficult. On the one hand, emphasis on a sense of common culture and identity suggests that nations that shared such attributes should increasingly gravitate together as allies, strengthening the increasing coalescence of like-minded nations into more integrated and internally coherent *civilizations*, as in Huntington's views of the future. To the extent that each civilization accepts the leadership of a core nation, the transition could result in the creation of a de facto centrally led coalition. But in the real world, it would not be that simple. Some outcomes are obvious: China would lead the Sinic bloc and Russia the Orthodox nations, although the greater autonomy afforded to the various Orthodox churches would compromise a common identity (the Russian Orthodox Church is at odds with the recently created Ukrainian Orthodox Church over political as well as religious issues). But who would lead the West? The United States, which de facto accepted the role during the Cold War, is declining in military and economic power in relative if not absolute terms, and shows little willingness to continue to assume the full burden of leadership. The European Union, initially cobbled together more for economic than geopolitical reasons, is internally riven with disputes rooted in long-standing economic and political differences. Who would play the role for Latin America or Africa? How would Japan or India fit in? Or the Muslim world, which traditionally lacks a core nation and is internally divided both by religious and secular conflicts? The point is that there is no simple and predictable answer. While it seems intuitively obvious that greater emphasis on identity and culture at the personal and national levels will reshape our view of the world, it is far more difficult to predict how the pieces will fit together.

The Possible Futures

When viewed from the perspective of the identity and culture paradigm, several possible alternative futures emerge (see table 4.1). They include:

- **the gradual emergence of a global identity and culture**, which transforms both personal and collective identity and alters the role of the nation-state and international institutions;

- **the merger of the identity-culture paradigm with the nation-state paradigm**, creating a fusion that can take several forms ranging from the benign rediscovery of national identity to the emergence of aggressive nations bent on asserting their sense of exceptionalism, inherent superiority, and dominance; and

Table 4.1. The Identity and Culture Paradigm

Global Identity and Culture	Identity and Culture Merge with the Nation-State	The Clash of Civilizations
A sense of global identity emerges, transcending previous national and cultural identities	Nation-states acquire increasing significance as agents of national identity and culture	The international system is built around civilizations, imposing a new sense of "tribal identity" and new "fault lines" of conflict
Increasing salience of and reliance on global and international institutions across a wide range of activities	Nation-states weaponize their sense of identity and culture to justify exceptionalism, manifest destiny, and imperialism	Nation-states maintain their significance as "core states" of a civilization or if they lie on "fault lines" on conflict
Decreasing salience of and reliance on the traditional nation-state, with less emphasis on sovereignty	The merger of the nation-state and identity/culture leads to disruptive internal political and social transformations and efforts to eliminate "foreign" influences	Conflict occurs between and within civilizations and at "fault lines" where they intersect
Acceptance of the leading role of global cities in setting cultural norms	Such nation-states seek to alter the international system, redefine the fault lines of conflict, and frequently export their sense of identity	International organizations and non-state actors will continue to exist in modified form, transformed by identity and culture
Acceptance of an expanding role for international civil society and NGOs	Such nations seek to redefine alliances and international organizations in terms of culture and identity	Conflict within and among civilizations will be difficult to mediate because of deep social and cultural roots

- the creation of an international system based on what Samuel Huntington has termed "the clash of civilizations," with the fault lines of major conflicts based on cultural differences.

THE GRADUAL EMERGENCE OF A GLOBAL IDENTITY AND CULTURE

In the gradual emergence of a global identity and culture, the emphasis should be on *gradual* because the world will not be changed overnight. Rather, change will come with the step-by-step realignment of the markers that define us and the social context within which we live. Traditional markers like race, religion, ethnicity, nationality, and the like will gradually become less salient, not so much forgotten as reinterpreted or supplanted by new elements of identity that seem more relevant in a rapidly changing world. We will not forget that we are French or American or Brazilian, but we will reinterpret these identities in light of an increasingly interconnected world. Economics will be an important part of it, but communications, entertainment, personal mobility, education, and the constant reinforcing presence of Walmarts, Starbucks, Volkswagens, and Hondas, things that remind us every day that we are a part of something far larger and diversified than it used to be.[5]

At the personal level, we will become the increasingly complex sum of more and more parts. In simpler days, our hyphenated identities were usually composed of just two important parts, as an African-American, a Polish-American, or a French-Canadian. An increasingly global world will become more complex as we try to cope with being, say, a Scotch-Irish-American professor married to a German-American spouse, with three children, two of whom are ethnically Chinese, educated in America and Russia, and living in a typical big university town in the middle of an overwhelmingly rural state. And I haven't even mentioned politics or religion. . . . Describing complex identities that way needs a lot more hyphens, and the order in which we arrange these markers constantly changes. The important point is that more and more of these markers enlarge our sense of what defines us, taking us beyond geographic and older cultural boundaries. We may not quite be citizens of the world, but we increasingly acknowledge that we are stakeholders in its fate.

What are the elements in this new sense of identity?[26] Most of the older ones—a traditional sense of national identity in geographic and cultural terms, ethnicity, religion, race, or political or class identity—will survive in modified form. New to the mix will be themes of universalization, secularization, pluralism, diversity, and tolerance, each having slightly different meanings in the cultures that adapt it. Taken together, they define a larger world and tell us how to fit in. Universalization and secularization suggest how our own identities and cultures will change; the definition of *us* stretches and becomes more inclusive, and the sense of *them* shrinks and becomes less exclusionary and menacing. There are more of *us* and fewer of *them*, and the differences now seem less important. Secularization and pluralism blunt the sharp edges that used to fundamentally divide us. While we still cling to beliefs, religions, ideologies, race, or ethnicity in defining our private selves, we increasingly accept that the broader public space in which we live has somehow agreed to set aside these considerations to create a secular playing field on which we all interact. To be sure, not without conflict, but now with new playbooks and rules of engagement that stress rule-governed and institutionalized ways of interacting and a tolerance for the legitimate interests that still divide us.

The Structure of Global Identity and Culture

A few caveats are necessary. First, it will not be a monoculture, not McWorld, as one author put it.[7] But there will be an ever-growing list of beliefs, institutions, and rules of engagement that appear in virtually all cultures, despite their remaining differences. Some will simply be repeated in each culture, embodied in that nation's laws like an amendment that standardizes or coordinates how we do things. Others will transcend cultures, penetrating more deeply into the underlying social and cultural fabric of all societies, something so basic that we almost do not need to write it down, like tolerance of diversity or the defense of human rights.

Second, a global identity and culture does not mean that a world government will emerge. To be sure, the traditional nation-state will be transformed, and the role of international and supranational bodies will grow. How and where we interact will change, reflecting the broader scope of our increasingly global identity and culture.

Third, the increasing importance of *global cities* must be acknowledged. Variously also called "megacities," "alpha cities," or "world cities," they play an increasingly important role as the catalysts for the emergence of a global identity and culture. They are the centers of economic power, financial services, corporate headquarters, technical and economic innovation, international trade, communications and media, cultural institutions like the theater and museums, and educational and research facilities. While they may have been important manufacturing centers in the past, their current ascendency is more closely tied to services. They are ethnically, linguistically, and culturally the most diverse places in the world. Over eight hundred languages and dialects are spoken in New York, with London a distant second at around three hundred. New York and London always top the various rankings, with Paris, Tokyo, Singapore, Amsterdam, Seoul, Berlin, Hong Kong, and Sydney completing the top ten. Other listings also include Shanghai and Dubai. Not surprisingly, the second-tier listing of up-and-coming global cities is even more diversified. By coincidence rather than by design, they are also usually the seats of government, but tellingly Washington, DC, Beijing, and Moscow don't make the first cut.[8]

In structural terms, a world of global identity and culture will be characterized by the transformation of the traditional Westphalian nation-state and the expanding role of international bodies. The nation-state will continue to exist as the primary structural building block of the international system, but the boundaries between what is purely domestic and what lies within the international realm will be less precisely drawn, just as the distinction between *us* and *them* will blur. It will de facto assert its de jure claim to sovereignty less and less, accepting greater international control or influence over economic, social, and humanitarian issues within its own borders. The global agenda will increasingly have impact on its own domestic priorities in areas like global warming, the environment, human rights, and other issues in which institutionalized global norms are increasingly embedded into international agreements and institutions. A common identity and culture will also affect how we deal with one another. Conflict avoidance and management practices will increasingly be based on the use of rule-based procedures and commonly accepted norms, and while that does not mean we will agree, it does give us a commonly accepted playbook on how we resolve our differences. A common sense of what is *fair* or *equitable* will haltingly emerge, as will a notion of individual and collective *social responsibility.*[9]

How Power Is Distributed in a World of Global Identity and Culture

Power is still very unevenly distributed in a world of global identity and culture. There will still be vast differences in the economic and military power among nations. A handful will still be at the top of the pecking order, although their relative power vis-à-vis one another may change. These will include the United States, still at the top in terms of absolute power, but slipping in terms of relative power, especially with the rise of China; China, whose economic growth will grow more rapidly than its military power; Russia, whose strongest card will remain military power, constantly diminished by its lagging technology and its even worse economy; Great Britain, whose place in the pecking order will be determined by the long-term fate of Brexit, but the outcome will probably range between bad (serious trade dislocations, with new ones gradually rebuilt) to very bad (new trade relations prove difficult to reestablish to fundamental political changes such as the unification of Ireland and Scottish independence); and France, whose economic and military power will decline relative to other top nations. That said, all five of these nations will maintain their veto-holding permanent seats in the UN Security Council.

The pecking order will be more diversified for the high-level second-tier nations that make up the G-20, which may expand. Some, like Japan, will maintain their economic power despite relative decline vis-à-vis

China and may play a greater regional or global military role. Germany will face the same dilemma in deciding how to leverage its economic power and play a greater international and perhaps military role. Others, like India or Indonesia, will surge ahead economically, while the rest will maintain a stable but not commanding presence in the global community.

Soft power will become more important in a world shaped by an expanding global identity and culture. While the top-tier nations will still have important advantages in asserting themselves, other nations will win respect and influence because of their evenhanded role as mediators or willingness to volunteer for peacekeeping and R2P activities.

Far more important is the way in which a growing sense of global identity and culture will internally transform the traditional Westphalian nation-state and existing international organizations. In the broadest sense, both will gradually converge around a widely accepted understanding about the role of the nation-states and international organizations. Nation-states will de facto and sometimes de jure accept reduced sovereignty at home and the growing impact of international organizations and commonly accepted international norms as global "best practices" that guide their action. International organizations and other multilateral rule-based organizations will gradually extend their impact by invasively asserting influence over what happens within once-sovereign nation-states or in the interactions among nation-states. Both processes will occur simultaneously and be mutually reinforcing, at least in theory. To be sure, there will be some rough spots and probably some reversals along the way, but the overall trend will be toward greater emphasis on the creation of a culture- and rule-based system of international interactions.

Sources of Stability and Instability

While the formal structures of the nation-state and international organizations will remain, stability will increasingly depend on how their citizens and members use them. To be sure, the day-to-day success of governments and economies will remain important. Prosperity, security, and stability will weigh heavily in determining what political scientists call "performance legitimacy," the acceptance of a set of political and economic relationships because they meet the tangible needs of everyday life. But now something further will be required: a sense of identity that is "bigger" or more inclusive, and a sense of holding a personal stake in the broader community that is emerging. It's something that most people will initially embrace with ambiguities and reservations—I'm still French (or whatever), but now I'm also European—but if it works and others embrace it along with you, it acquires momentum and increasing acceptance. It becomes the "new normal," inconceivable a decade ago but now just a part of the broader world in which you live.

It will not survive on its own, and it is reversible if things go badly. Many other things will be needed: political stability within nation-states and relative peace among them; nations that are willing to lead the transformation, and others that are willing to follow; the management of revisionist and rogue nations, especially those not in tune with the emerging consensus; an acceptable level of prosperity and widespread if not universal acceptance of the distribution of wealth and power; increasingly open and tolerant cultures that embrace change; and a sense of personal and collective security in one's new identity and culture.

The potential sources of instability are also numerous: political unrest within nations; the revival of older and divisive identities and cultures; wars or the creation of alliances and blocs that undercut a sense of common identity; economic crises; a widespread backlash against all that is new and different; or a revolution of rising expectations that creates impossible hopes and demands on new ideas and institutions—all create potential instabilities that could overpower the fledgling sense of common identity and culture.

Catastrophic and unanticipated events may also challenge the stability of a nascent sense of a global identity and culture. Uncommonly protracted wars or other conflicts, especially if they produce extensive economic and social dislocations, will undercut the perception of a common culture and challenge the political and social institutions that have identified with its creation. Widespread migrations spawned by economic dislocations, famines, pandemics, or natural disasters will also impact on the new sense of world order.

The response to such shocks to the system could go in several different directions. If the challenge were perceived as universally or at least widely affecting the entire international community, a common response could occur. A sense of "We're all in this together" would deepen the commitment to joint action, probably strengthening those within nation-states committed to such collaboration and increasing the impact and credibility of multilateral and global institutions that would be at the forefront of the common response. The UN and its agencies such as the World Health Organization, other entities such as the World Trade Organization, or those associated with the Paris Agreement on climate change could rise to the occasion, hopefully demonstrating the wisdom of a common perception and action.

But it could go in a different direction, especially if the challenges were perceived as not universally affecting the global community or if nation-states fell into a blame game about who was responsible for the problem. Some problems are simply more inherently local than others; civil or localized wars, floods or other natural disasters, or other disruptions may not equally impact all members of the international community. "Not my problem" or "You brought this on yourself" will become tempting responses if the problems seem distant, and such responses will undercut both the social and institutional commitment to rising to the challenge of somebody else's disaster. Conversely, some problems are universal virtually by definition; *pan*demics eventually span the globe, as do issues of global warming and environmental degradation. But even the deepest philosophical commitment to a sense of global identity and common risk will be challenged by the politically inevitable temptation to fix one's own problems at home before responding to the needs of neighbors or distant nations.

What Would a World Based on Global Identity and Culture Look Like?

We have already seen halting and incomplete efforts to create an international system built upon shared norms, each ultimately ending in failure as new fault lines and conflicts emerged. In one sense, European political elites before World War I lived at least partially in such a world. Intermarriage among the royal families, a common sense of religion rooted in various interpretations of Christianity, and a common elite culture based on wealth, privilege, and access to political power created as least a semblance of cultural unity.[10] There also was a widespread assumption that this elite agreed on the terms of engagement embodied in the balance of power system created at the Congress of Vienna in 1815. What could go wrong?

World War I answered that question: everything. By the end of the war, empires, monarchies, institutions, and the sense of a common culture collapsed. The revolution that tore through Russia offered a totally different version of a future global culture based on economics and ideology, not traditional notions of identity and culture. The Versailles Conference tried to piece things back together. The new postwar culture would be based on the progressive notions of democracy and national self-determination, institutionalized through the creation of parliamentary democracies in most of the new nations that had been carved out of the Austro-Hungarian, Russian, and Ottoman Empires. International conflicts would be solved through collective security and the League of Nations, aided by efforts to punish German aggression and maintain arms control. Russia, now the Soviet Union, would be excluded from the new arrangements in the hope that the regime would crumble and the problem simply go away. The Americans, newcomers to the game during the war, went home and decided not to join the League. It proved impossible to create a new sense of identity and culture that might unite Europe and North America. National self-determination stoked even greater identification with old divisive allegiances, and the hodgepodge of new and frequently unstable nation-states empowered conflicts. Most of the new democracies in Europe failed, discrediting the concept of popular rule, and were replaced by right-wing dictatorships or military rule. The sense of identity and culture fragmented into combative ethnic, national, or religious differences, abetted by ideological distinctions along the entire spectrum from far left to far right.[11]

Post–World War II efforts to rebuild a viable international system focused primarily on the nuts-and-bolts issues rather than on the creation of a common sense of identity and culture. Emphasis fell on creating a workable and far more realistic collective security system in the United Nations and international trade and stability through the Bretton Woods initiatives. Efforts to create viable democracies, especially in Germany and Japan, were based more on military occupation and barely concealed American intervention rather than on less tangible efforts to create a democratic political culture, although that was a long-term goal. While the Cold War sharpened the fault lines between East and West, the distinctions were drawn in geopolitical and ideological terms rather than traditional cultural differences.

The end of the Cold War provided a brief period of optimism that now a truly universal culture might emerge, aided in no small part by the simultaneous emergence of a nascent global economy and the impact of global cities, communications, entertainment, travel, and (for better or worse) the ubiquitous presence of all the Walmarts, Carrefours, McDonald's, and the rest. Even if you could not agree on whether the geopolitical structure of this new world order was hegemonic or multipolar, much less who led it, it did seem for a while that most of the old fault lines were gone or significantly less important. There were a number of hopeful signs that perhaps movement toward a global culture, supported by an increasingly global economy, might make a lasting difference. These included a seeming consensus around the central importance of liberal democracy and market economies, backstopped by the creation of post–Cold War democratic regimes in the former Soviet states and Eastern Europe; the increasing political as well as economic integration of the EU, and near universal membership in the WTO; the institutionalization of broad international agreements about human rights, environmental concerns and global warming; and the creation of precedent-setting institutions such as the International Criminal Court, whose members surrendered considerable sovereignty in order to punish war crimes and genocide.

That didn't last long. Perhaps inevitably, conflicts and fault lines reemerged, sometimes driven by the tangible metrics of national rivalries (the rise of China as an economic and military power, the reemergence of Russia, and the ambivalent status and role of the United States) but also increasingly linked to the growing salience of issues linked to identity and culture. Huntington's prediction of a "clash of civilizations" was both a prediction and a warning. More ominously, battles over identity and culture not only drew the sort of international fault lines Huntington mentioned, but they also divided nations internally, threatening to upset and redefine partisan identities and were linked to other divisive issues of race, gender, generational conflicts, international migration, and the growing divide between the haves and have-nots.

THE IDENTITY AND CULTURE PARADIGM MERGES WITH THE NATION-STATE PARADIGM: IDENTITY ACQUIRES A POTENT INSTITUTIONAL FORM

The discovery or reanimation of a sense of identity and culture merges with older notions of the nation-state, creating a new and usually politically volatile force that reshapes domestic politics and the international system. In one sense, it is an aggressive reaffirmation of a sense of patriotism, a fusion of a sense of being different from others and a sense of pride in that difference. It can take many institutional forms, ranging from a benign feeling that "We're different" to a more virulent assertion that "We're superior and entitled to aggressively assert that superiority, both at home and abroad." Frequently it takes the form of the rediscovery of a previous sense of national identity and culture, whose superiority and purity are exaggerated through the rose-colored glasses of historical memory. "We used to be united around a sense common identity and purpose, but now. . . . What happened, and how do we reclaim that sense of unity and purpose?" If the answer is simply that we've collectively forgotten, distracted by our own preoccupations of living in an ahistorical world, the solution is easy, but perhaps internally disruptive. We need to rediscover that identity among ourselves. It's our problem, and it's our task to work it out.

Frequently it's not that simple. If the answer is that our identity has been taken away from us by foreign invasion, by a revolution that failed to create a new identity, or by social change brought on by economic diversification and immigration, the task of redefining ourselves will be more difficult and combative. The redefinition will be all the more difficult if there is a sense of victimization or betrayal. Now there are *others* among *us*, and we are going to have to figure out how to deal with that. Even worse, perhaps certain elements of our own people have lost touch with our "true" sense of national identity, unwittingly or consciously misleading us, perhaps for their own benefit. The reanimation of that older sense of identity rapidly takes on political form, sometimes but not always subsumed under the term "populism."[12] New movements or political parties emerge, challenging whatever had been the conventional wisdom and institutional order of the "old" politics. New charismatic leaders emerge, frequently from the fringes of the old order, and build broadly supported coalitions of voters who feel abandoned and betrayed. Identity and culture become what political scientists call "wedge issues," intensely disputed questions that split apart old alignments and institutions and redefine how and why the game is played. It is likely to be particularly disruptive in newly created democracies, especially those simultaneously experiencing economic and social instability. But even the seemingly most stable democracies like those of Great Britain, France, and the United States are not immune.

The Structure of the Identity and Nation-State International System
There are essentially two variations to the fusion of the identity and nation-state paradigms: (1) a relatively benign rediscovery of a sense of national identity and culture, animating a new sense of national unity and pride, and (2) the more disruptive "weaponized" version in which the struggle over identity transforms the political, economic, and social structure of the nation, often with deep implications for how it fits into

the larger international system. Lithuania will provide a good example of the former, and France, Great Britain, and Turkey of the latter.

Variation One: Lithuania—"We're Back, Much As We Were"

Lithuania, like the other Baltic states of Latvia and Estonia, has a long history as a coherent independent culture and sometimes as a separate nation-state.[13] Given its independence by the Versailles Treaty after World War I, it survived as an independent nation until 1939, when a secret agreement between Hitler's Germany and Stalin's Soviet Union divided the Baltic States and brought them under German and Soviet control. After World War II, with the Red Army in charge, Lithuania and the other Baltic States were incorporated into the Soviet Union. Moscow firmly controlled the Lithuanian Communist Party, which firmly controlled all political life. While it was formally led by ethnically Lithuanian communists, Moscow called the shots.

That began to change when Mikhail Gorbachev came to power in the Soviet Union in 1985. With rumors of change in the air, especially for the non-Russian republics of the Soviet Union, the Lithuanians and others began to test the waters. Cautiously at first, they raised issues of culture and history, which emboldened further demands for greater autonomy, and perhaps more. The debate initially divided the Lithuanian Communist Party into pro-Moscow and nativist wings. Soon the broadly based popular front Sajudis was formed to incorporate the rapidly growing independence movement, joined by both communist and non-communist elements. Former communist leaders quickly rediscovered their ethnic roots and joined the common front. The first democratic election was held in 1990, sweeping Sajudis into power. Lithuania proclaimed its independence even before the Soviet Union broke up in December 1991.

Lithuania quickly returned to its pre-war democratic roots, creating a mixed presidential-parliamentary system in which the unicameral legislature, the Seimas, and the president are independently elected. The prime minister, who runs the government on a day-to-day basis, is nominated by the president and approved by the legislature. In the first decade after independence, power was fairly evenly divided between Conservatives, the stronghold of the popular front that led the fight for independence, and the Democratic Labor Party, a reconstituted version of the former communist party, now espousing European-style social democracy. The emergence of a powerful centrist coalition and a number of smaller parties in the 2000 election altered the pattern. Now the norm sees the creation of multiparty coalitions usually built around the two strongest plurality parties, the Homeland Union—Lithuanian Christians Democrats and the Farmers and Greens Union—and including the Social Democrats and/or the Liberal Movement. In the 2019 presidential election, both of the leading candidates who made it into the second-round runoff ran as independents, a pattern that is likely to continue. All and all, it is normal multiparty politics in a presidential-parliamentary regime, with all of the expected suspense, political wheeling and dealing, and occasional scandals that characterize a functioning democracy in the real world.

An important part of understanding why the transition was so peaceful lies in what didn't happen—the fate of the Russian minority never became a disruptive issue. In 1991, just under 10 percent of the population was ethnically Russian, many purposely transplanted to strengthen Moscow's control. By 2015, the number had fallen to 4.8 percent, mostly attributable to voluntary relocation. Even during the high point of Russian presence, Lithuanians were more tolerant of the Russians living among them than the other Baltic States' populations. Most importantly, in the post-communist era, the issue was never weaponized, neither by the Lithuanians themselves nor by the remaining Russians, who felt endangered by their minority status. To be sure, there certainly were frictions and a few show trails, largely in absentia. But by and large, the past remained in the past.

Variation Two: First Example: France—"There Are Many Versions of France"

Since the revolution of 1789, France has been internally divided by multiple and usually conflicted identities. Many were rooted in unresolved political issues of who should govern. The revolutionary regime was replaced by the First Empire under Napoleon I, followed by two attempts to restore the monarchy under Bourbon and then Orleans kings. That eventually ended with the rise of the Second Empire under Napoleon III, which yielded to the Third Republic after France was defeated by Germany in the Franco-Prussian War in 1871. The Fourth Republic came along after World War II, and the current Fifth Republic in the late 1950s under Charles de Gaulle.

France's conflicted identities also were deeply rooted in culture and religion. Regional identities have always been significant, even as the growing power of the central government in Paris and the impact of industrialization spread across the land. The urban-rural distinction remains strong even today, in part because of a sense of "peasant romanticism" and the economic reality that the agricultural sector remains far larger than in most other industrialized nations of Europe. Roman Catholicism remains a strong point of identity for many French, although the political power of the Church waned, especially after World War II. Historically a sense of Catholic identity was not pitted against Protestant denominations or other religions but against a strong sense of secularism, a major theme of public life since the revolution.

Immigration also played an important role in animating an increasingly acrimonious debate over French identity. Immigrants from former French colonies were the first wave in the 1960s and 1970s, followed by an even greater influx due to worker migration within the European Union and its earlier Common Market arrangements, and then by refugees, largely from the Middle East and Africa, in recent years. Keeping with the notions of secularization and the creation of a common French identity, the newcomers were expected to "fit in," gradually surrendering whatever identities they brought with them and becoming a part of the French melting pot. Some did, especially among the earliest immigrants, but most didn't, setting the stage for a deeper confrontation.

That confrontation, which has upended the once stable party alignments of the Fifth Republic and redefined the nature of French politics, began simply enough with the creation of a traditional right-wing party in 1972 called the National Front, led by Jean-Marie Le Pen.[14] One of many niche parties on the right, it initially focused on vague issues of national identity. It did poorly. By the late 1980s the political landscape had begun to change. The issue of French identity now acquired a more specific focus: the growing influx of immigrants, especially Muslims, and their impact on the culture and economy. The *other* was among *us*, taking our jobs, challenging our religion and culture, and refusing to "fit in," the long-standing price of acceptance of previous immigrants—all the classic elements needed to weaponize a new issue into a game-changing political movement. Support for the National Front grew slowly, at first in a few secondary cities and regional bodies, and in the European Parliament, where new parties sometimes make their first mark.

The real breakthrough occurred in the 2002 presidential election, in which the polls predicted a runoff between the incumbent, President Jacques Chirac, leader of the Gaullists, the center-right heirs to the legacy of Charles de Gaulle, and Lionel Jospin, leader of the Socialist Party. Le Pen edged out Jospin in the first round, forcing a runoff between him and Chirac. Shocked by results, the establishment parties of right and left united behind Chirac, who won with 82 percent, with 71 percent of his votes cast simply to block Le Pen.

Le Pen found it difficult to capitalize on his newfound support. The right-wing forces remained divided among themselves, and the National Front fared poorly in subsequent local and regional elections. In the 2007 presidential elections, Le Pen won only 11 percent of first-round votes. In the following year, he announced his intention to step down from the leadership in 2010, provoking a battle over the choice of his successor and the future role of the party.

Marine Le Pen, his daughter, won control of the party and set out to soften its xenophobic image and to bring it more into the political mainstream, focusing on anti-EU, anti-establishment, put-France-first, and law-and-order issues as well as immigration. She further underscored her intention to forge a new identity by forcing her father to break all ties with the party he had created. As the party's 2012 presidential candidate, she got 18 percent of the first-round votes. Over the next several years, the party did better in local and regional elections, aided by its growing acceptance as a mainstream party and by increasing public concern over immigration and economic issues. In the 2017 presidential election, Le Pen received 21 percent in the first round, second only to Emmanuel Macron's 24 percent. In the second round, Macron, himself a nontraditional candidate running under the banner of the newly created En Marche Party, won with 66 percent of the vote. For the first time in the history of the Fifth Republic, a runoff presidential election occurred without a candidate of either of the old-line mainstream parties in contention. French politics had been changed, the credit or blame going to a once-upstart fringe party that learned how to weaponize the issues of identity and culture.

Variation Two: Second Example: Great Britain—"A Place of Different Parts"

Britain's formal legal name is the United Kingdom of Great Britain and Northern Ireland. Historically, getting all of that together and keeping it together has not been easy. Strong regional identities have always been there, and for many the "regions" are really separate nations uneasily (and perhaps unfairly) cobbled together into a formal union of many different parts. Some of that belongs in distant history (the subjugation of Wales in 1707 or the formal union of England and Scotland in the same year), but much of it is recent history (the partition of Ireland into the separate Republic of Ireland and Northern Ireland, which remained in the UK, and the "devolution" of power from London to separate parliaments in Scotland, Wales, and Northern Ireland, mostly in the 1990s). The most recent chapter begins with membership in the European Union in 1972.

Getting in had not been easy or uncontested. Entry had been blocked by the French until after de Gaulle left office in 1969. Formal entry, subsequently approved by a referendum in 1975, left the Labour Party and a growing group of "Eurosceptics" among the Conservatives still in opposition. The Maastricht Treaty, signed in 1993, turned what had been an economic free trade area into a fledgling political union, stoking concern that the nation's sovereignty had been compromised. Right-wing resistance among the Tories grew, and a new party, the United Kingdom Independence Party (UKIP), was formed under the leadership of Nigel Farage.

British membership in the EU brought many changes, many of them perceived as threatening. While London flourished as a major center of trade and commerce, the traditional industrial regions languished. Technologically obsolescent industries could not complete with the more advanced producers in Europe and Asia, and the free flow of labor brought in a large number of low-wage workers from Eastern Europe, followed by an influx of immigrants from the Middle East and Africa. As in France, the *other* was now among *us*, taking our jobs and changing our culture. UKIP soon discovered the value of weaponizing the issue, as had the National Front in France, increasingly becoming an anti-immigrant, anti-EU, and antiestablishment party and a haven for those who felt abandoned or betrayed.

Responding to a growing sense of regional identity in Scotland, Wales, and Northern Ireland in the late 1990s, the central government in London began a process of "devolution"—the transfer of greater control of local affairs to newly created local parliaments. Intended to reduce growing separatist demands, it did exactly the opposite, also signaling the weakness of the central government at a time when opposition to continued EU membership was growing.

The Scottish National Party soon won control of the local government in Scotland, virtually destroying what had been Labour Party dominance in the region and undercutting Labour's power in Parliament in London. A referendum on Scottish independence followed in 2014, with 55 percent voting to remain in the United Kingdom and 45 percent voting to leave. Defeated for now, those who wanted to leave vowed that the issue would not go away.

Conservative prime minister David Cameron, hoping to win the support of the right-wing Eurosceptics within his own party and attract voters from UKIP in the approaching 2015 parliamentary election, pledged that his government would hold a referendum on continued EU membership if returned to office. Win they did, and he was forced to honor his promise, hoping that a defeat for the "leavers" would settle the issue. It did, but not in the way Cameron had hoped.[15]

The voting took place on June 23, 2016; 51.9 percent of the country voted to leave the EU, and 48.1 percent voted to remain. Hardly a landslide, but a decision nonetheless, one that would shake Parliament and the party system to its core. Cameron resigned, replaced by fellow Tory Theresa May, who vainly attempted to negotiate a departure agreement acceptable to the EU and Parliament. It was not to be....

Those voting to leave were a predictable collection of self-proclaimed victims of free trade: older, less educated and low-income voters, typically living in those areas in England that had been hollowed out by foreign competition and de-industrialization and had experienced the greatest influx of foreign workers. Joining them were voters from the more traditional Tory right, primarily concerned with the preservation of the nation's sovereignty and traditional culture rather than bread-and-butter concerns. London voted overwhelmingly to stay. England and Wales voted to leave, while Scotland and Northern Ireland voted overwhelmingly to stay.

In March 2017, Prime Minister May began the formal process of withdrawal. The talks proved difficult for many reasons. London had hoped to preserve much of the free trade structure that gave it access to European markets while closing the door to further immigration of foreign workers. The EU refused, taking a hardline, all-or-nothing position. Disagreement on how Northern Ireland would fit into the new arrangement also stalled the talks. Eurosceptics within the Conservative Party denied May a majority for her proposals, and more radical figures began to argue for withdrawal without a formal agreement.

Facing strong opposition, May called a snap election in June 2017, hoping to win greater support in Commons. Exactly the opposite happened, and the Tories lost their slim majority and were now forced to rule as a minority government, with the occasional support of the Democratic Unionist Party of Northern Ireland. May resigned in July 2019, replaced by Boris Johnson, the former mayor of London who championed withdrawal without a formal agreement, if necessary. In December, Johnson called an early general election, and the Tories won a commanding majority. London and the EU cobbled together a mutually acceptable agreement, a document that left many of the nuts-and-bolts details for further talks.

Variation Two: Third Example: Turkey—"Secular and Religious Identity Uneasily Coexist"

Modern Turkey emerged from the breakup of the Ottoman Empire at the end of World War I. Long described as "the sick man of Europe," the empire was deeply rooted in the political and social structure of Ottoman society. Political and religious leadership were vested in the sultan, who also functioned as the caliph, the head of the dominant Sunni Muslim community. Society was organized into a series of *millets*, distinctive communities based on ethnicity, religion, occupation, or other differences, whose members were clearly identifiable because of their unique clothing or other markers. While there had been some attempts to Westernize the empire before World War I, all failed in the face of political and religious opposition. By 1924, a reform movement coalesced around the leadership of Mustafa Kemal, a prominent military leader, who eventually took the additional name Ataturk, "Father of the Turks," to signify his role as the creator of a modern Western and secular state. His reforms touched all aspects of Turkish life. The Ottoman Empire was dissolved, and the positions of sultan and caliph were abolished. An elected legislature, the Grand National Assembly, was created, which would choose a president and prime minister to lead the nation. From 1923 to 1945, only one political party, the Ataturk-led Republican People's Party, dominated political life. Rapid economic growth was promised, to be implemented through a series of five-year plans and closer ties with more advanced Western nations. The educational system was reformed along Western lines, and European legal codes were adopted. Even more significantly, cultural and social reforms profoundly transformed the nation. Western modes of dress and social conduct were adopted. The Arabic-scripted Turkish language shifted to a modified Latin alphabet, and the nation adopted the Gregorian calendar.

More important was the impact on religion. While freedom of religion was firmly established, the state was to become secular and neutral on all religious issues. Religiously based *millets* were abolished and other religious organizations were instructed to work within the parameters of secular rule. Opposition to secularization was suppressed, and the army assumed the special role of protector of Ataturk's reforms, most importantly the separation between religion and the state.[16]

The consensus that supported Ataturk's reforms remained reasonably stable even after his death in 1938. After World War II a multiparty system was introduced. In 1950, the election of a Democratic Party government marked the emergence of an increasingly competitive system. Turkish political life steadily became more combative, prompting the military to intervene on four occasions either to force the resignation of civilian authorities or to establish direct, if temporary, military rule. The growing discord spanned the full range of economic and social issues, eventually raising the key question of the role of religion in political life.

In 2002, a series of economic shocks resulted in the election of a government controlled by the moderately conservative Justice and Development Party, headed by Recep Tayyip Erdogan, the former mayor of Istanbul. Although it initially endorsed membership in the European Union, the increasingly conservative party began to raise issues that supported a reconsideration of Ataturk's Western and secular model for the nation, putting it on a collision course with the military, which reaffirmed its guardian role over the nation's future. To be sure, neither the party nor Erdogan personally were anywhere near being Muslim extremists like ISIS or Al-Qaeda, and the issues that roiled Turkish politics in the coming years included questions such as the powers vested in the presidency, personal rivalries among party leaders, and the usual assortment of economic and foreign policy issues. But as the party's and Erdogan's popularity rose, both moved to increasingly endorse the acceptability of some elements of traditional Turkish culture and to question the commitment to a purely secular state.

The party's popularity grew steadily, bringing Erdogan first to the post of prime minister from 2003 to 2014 and then to the presidency in 2014. He quickly began to play a more assertive and confrontational role as president, bringing the press and the courts more under government control and reintroducing many of the ceremonial aspects of the Ottoman tradition.[17]

On July 15, 2016, a faction within the military attempted a coup d'état, citing the erosion of secular rule, human rights, and democracy as the reason for their action. They briefly seized control of small portions of Istanbul and Ankara and attacked other military installations. An attempt to capture or assassinate Erdogan failed. It was over quickly. Erdogan quickly and brutally reestablished even firmer control over the military, thoroughly purging it of any real or potential opposition. Similar purges swept through the media, academe, and any other institution that had not risen to support Erdogan at the moment of crisis.

The following year, Erdogan secured the passage of a constitutional amendment that fundamentally strengthened the presidency. The president would be directly elected rather than chosen by the legislature, and the office of prime minister would be eliminated. The new presidency is modeled on the American office, with strong executive powers given to the incumbent. The referendum to approve the changes passed with 51.4 percent of the popular vote, signaling continuing opposition to Erdogan's increasingly authoritarian ways and his vision of Turkey's future. A year later in the 2018 presidential election Erdogan was returned to office by a similarly narrow margin, 53 percent of the popular vote.

Undaunted, Erdogan has continued to implement policies that restore at least a symbolic recognition of past Ottoman glories, possibly to strengthen support within his conservative and religious base in the face of growing economic problems and the victory of opposition parties in the municipal elections in Istanbul and Ankara. In 2020, he won permission from the courts to restore the Hagia Sophia, the iconic domed structure that dominates Istanbul's skyline, to the status of a functioning mosque. Since its creation in the sixth century, it has been an Eastern Orthodox cathedral, a Roman Catholic cathedral, a mosque, and under Ataturk, a secular museum. Now, once again, it's a mosque. The past and the future are still at war to define the nation's identity.

How Power Is Distributed in a World in Which Identity and Nation-States Merge

How power is distributed in a world in which identity and nation-states merge is simple and predictable: in institutional terms, it flows to the nation-states themselves, which emerge as even more powerful players in the international system. Nation-states get a new breath of life, at least to the extent that the rebirth of identity strengthens national unity and a widespread commitment to a government that defends it both at home and abroad. A sense of exceptionalism and aggressive "us first" policies undercut broader commitments to globalization, international organizations, and multinational efforts. Emphasis now falls on one-on-one transactional diplomatic and trade agreements, especially with other nations that are "like us," whatever that means. Conversely, international organizations or other multilateral arrangements become less important. To be sure, a degree of reality will remain: powerful nations like the United States, China, or Russia can indulge themselves in rediscovering their national identity, safe in the reality that they will remain important global powers. Others may not be that lucky. As an independent nation once again, Lithuania returned to the role of sovereign state, albeit a minor one, with no illusions about what that means. France remains France, a major European power but a high second-tier power on the larger global stage. The impact of Brexit on Great Britain is harder to predict, in part because of its economic and military implications and in part because of the possibility of Scottish independence and the unification of Ireland.

The reanimation of a sense of national identity and culture also may stoke seemingly dormant international conflicts or invent completely new ones. In one sense, the old confrontations of the Cold War are returning, now cloaked in terms of national or cultural fault lines. The confrontation between the United States and Russia, largely absent from the world stage until the Cold War, seems to be returning in a different but predictable form as a geopolitical issue tied to an assertion of the exceptionalism of Russian Orthodox culture. In a similar form, American-Chinese hostilities, once couched in Cold War and ideological terms, now increasingly play out as a geopolitical and economic confrontation between a rapidly advancing nation and a status quo and declining nation, and as a clash between what Huntington terms the Sinic and Western civilizations. The same may potentially occur within the EU, based upon conflicting French, German, or Italian interests, or more broadly between the "old" Europe (the Cold War era economic and military alliance members) and the "new" Europe (the broader and more heterogeneous EU membership including East European nations no longer under Moscow's control).

Sources of Stability and Instability

Bluntly put, the stability of the international system will be difficult to sustain in a world of newly empowered nation-states eager to assert their identity and culture. As with all of our versions of international systems, a major component of stability lies in the relationship among the major powers. The prospects are not good on that score, neither in terms of domestic stability within each major power nor the stability of the formal and informal arrangements that govern their interaction. Some but not all of that stems from a reassertion of national identity. Under the Trump administration, for example, the United States is seeking to redefine the American role in the world, provoking puzzlement, anger, and opposition from traditional allies. American domestic politics seems to have entered new and uncharted waters, with the traditional parties (the Democrats, heading a center-left coalition, and the Republicans leading a center-right counterpart) now under challenge from both right and left.

Partisanship aside, no one can predict where this is headed and how it will affect America's role in the world. Great Britain faces the same confusion and conflicted reality; the firestorm ignited by Brexit has not yet run its course, and no one really knows the full outcome. While French domestic politics has been roiled by the rise of the National Rally and Macron's En Marche, suggesting a fundamental realignment of the party system, it has maintained its commitment to globalization and the broader outlines of the post–Cold War international system. Germany has been the bedrock of stability in Europe, but no one can be sure what will happen when Angela Merkel leaves office. China and Russia, each endorsing the growing importance of aggressive national identity in its own way, now play the more predictable role of a rising (or returning) major power intent on challenging the previous world order in geopolitical, economic, and cultural terms.

Such dangers will not be limited to the major powers. The fusion of an aggressive national culture and an assertive (and probably better armed) nation-state will have impact elsewhere. In the Middle East, the endless sectarian conflicts between Sunni and Shiite Muslims will be exacerbated by national rivalries between would-be regional hegemons like Saudi Arabia and Iran, to say nothing of the continuing impact of the Palestinian question and the brooding presence of terrorist forces. In South Asia, Indian nationalism and Hindu assertiveness will intensify the dangerous standoff between India and Pakistan, as will the apparent Indian seizure of half of Jammu and Kashmir. And so it goes, but now with the important caveat that the peacekeeping role of the major powers or international organizations may be far more difficult to play because of the growing direct conflicts among the former and the weakening of the latter.

Catastrophic events such as the social and economic impact of civil or local wars, famines, widespread migration, earthquakes, floods, and a host of other natural or manmade disasters will play out within the same context. The empowerment of a sense of national and cultural distinctiveness, as well as a disruptive dose of aggressive exceptionalism, will undercut efforts to find broadly supported responses at the regional or global level. Multilateral agencies such as the United Nations as well as others targeted at economic, medical, or other humanitarian relief efforts will be compromised by the growing sense of "my country first." Organizations like Doctors Without Borders will quickly learn that borders are ever more important in a world that links and prioritizes mutually reinforcing national and cultural distinctiveness. While, in some sense, continuing membership in a broader community may remain as "special relationships" that allegedly link nations such as the United States and the United Kingdom (with Canada and sometimes Australia added as junior partners) and the Commonwealth of Nations (made up of fifty-four very different nations that emerged from the breakup of the British empire), or a sense of affinity that links France with some of its former colonies, especially in Francophone Africa, such relationships are likely to be sorely tested by a strengthened commitment to nationalism and cultural distinctiveness.

What Would a World Based on an Aggressive Merger of Identity and Culture with Traditional Nation-States Look Like?

What would a world based on an aggressive merger of identity and culture with traditional nation-states look like? You don't have to look far for the answer. It's all around you, because that merger is one of the major forces reshaping the international system today. To be sure, it's not the only one. Economic factors or ideology also play a role, as the other chapters indicate. Issues like global warming, the environment, human rights, migration, pandemics, and resource depletion are also on the list, as are the impact of new technologies, especially in communications, travel, and conventional and nuclear weaponry. But those issues aside, the major political issue driving the changing nature of the international system is the emergence and, in the most disruptive cases, the weaponization of issues linking identity and culture to newly empowered and aggressive nation-states. Much of it probably was an inevitable backlash to the impact of economic and cultural globalization and the growing role of new political entities like the EU and multinational bodies such as the WTO and multinational corporations. But that was only a part of the story. Important also was the politically seductive discovery that weaponizing these issues could be a game-changing factor in winning political power at home and dislodging the establishment, international elites, the powers that be, the one percent, or whatever you call them. Like any successful political appeal, identity and culture become deeply emotional battle cries in the mouths of those who feel left behind, belittled, ignored, and powerless. Fear and anger win elections and build broad public support, and they sustain and carry to victory those who know how to weaponize them. What we don't know is whether this disruptive marriage of convenience between identity and the revival of powerful nation-states is a short-term liaison or a long-term relationship, the new normal of the international system. If the former, it will still make significant changes in the international system, but decrease in importance as new issues and political strategies emerge. If the latter, the international system may move toward a full-fledged "clash of civilizations," as Huntington predicts.

THE CREATION OF AN INTERNATIONAL SYSTEM BASED ON THE "CLASH OF CIVILIZATIONS"

In many ways the formal structure of the international system will be the same, composed primarily of nation-states, international organizations, and an assortment of bilateral and/or multilateral agreements that deal with a broad spectrum of issues. The important difference will be the nature of the issues that divide them, what motivates them to action, and the way in which they interact within a redefined international system. The driving forces will be the perceived differences between the world's major cultures, giving rise to what Huntington calls "tribal conflict on a global scale."[18] Nation-states and all of the other formal organizations of the international system will be reconceptualized and animated by their role as actors within that broader struggle. They will make sense only within the context of that broader framework, as leaders or followers within each "civilization," acting out situational roles already largely defined for them and choosing enemies and allies within that context.

Important roles will fall to "core states" or states that exist on "fault lines" that define cultural boundaries. In the simplest configuration, core states will be recognized as the most critical in defining what a particular culture means and, hopefully, its most powerful advocates or defenders on the global stage. That means one widely accepted core state for each culture, and agreement on its interpretation of what the culture means and its tactical choices in defending it—hardly a likely outcome in the real world. Fault-line states are on the front lines, where the *other* is just across the border. Even worse, the line of demarcation may run through a particular nation-state, or enclaves of *them* may live among *us* or vice versa.

The Structure of a World Defined by the "Clash of Civilizations"
Huntington divides the post–Cold War world into eight "civilizations," some more clearly articulated than others:

1. Sinic, or Chinese civilization, including the areas traditionally dominated by a unified China but internally divided by long-standing regional, linguistic, and religious differences (including Buddhism, Taoism, Confucianism, Christianity, and efforts to create a secular culture after the communist revolution in 1948);

2. Japanese civilization, a distinctive offshoot of Chinese culture from 100 CE onward, and internally divided by the Buddhist and Shinto religions;

3. Hindu civilization of India, split by sharp regional and cultural divisions prior to British colonization and subsequently by the clash between Hindus and Muslims after independence;

4. Islamic civilization, originating in the Middle East but with significant Muslim communities in South Asia, Indonesia, Malaysia, and internally divided by significant differences between Sunni and Shiite communities and their subgroups and by important secular and political issues;

5. Orthodox civilization, traditionally identified by affiliation with the Greek or Russian Orthodox churches, but also present as Orthodox communities in central and southern Europe, and internally divided by the liturgical independence of each Orthodox community and by secular and political differences;

6. Latin American civilization, a combination of what remains of the indigenous pre-colonial cultures in South and Central America and the European culture brought by Spanish and Portuguese settlers, and internally divided by national and secular cultural differences;

7. African civilization, the most tenuous of Huntington's categories, centered on sub-Saharan Africa and divided by long-standing pre-colonial political, religious, and cultural differences and by the differing impact of British, French, Belgian, and German colonialism; and

8. Western civilization, initially based in Western Europe and then spread to North and South America, but also with impact on the colonial empires of the major European powers, and supported by the impact of Christianity and the industrial revolution, but divided by long-standing cultural and geopolitical differences and divisions between Catholic and Protestant interpretations of Christianity.

While Huntington's outline of potentially contending civilizations provides an overview of cultural differences, it is much harder to translate it into a concrete map of opposing forces. In the real world of the twenty-first century, cultural boundaries are fuzzy, to say the least. Even what seem to be the clearest distinctions—religion and ethnic identity—fail to draw clear boundaries in terms of the nature of the international system. While specific examples may illustrate such divisions—the treatment of Muslim Rohingya in Buddhist Myanmar, or the hodgepodge of religious and ethnic clashes that followed the breakup of Yugoslavia, for example—it is difficult to explain all international disputes in similar terms. Moreover, civilizations and cultures are hardly internally monolithic. All religions are rife with internal schisms and sects whose differences are deadly serious to the true believers, and all cultures generate endless arguments about their traditional or modern manifestations. And not all believers internalize religion, culture, or ethnicity as deeply as others; for some, they become the central and defining core of their existence, while for others they are only a small part of a larger picture.

How Power Is Distributed in a World of Clashing Civilizations

The explanation of how power is distributed in a world of clashing civilizations comes in several parts. First, nation-states will remain the most powerful entities in the international system. But now their influence will be determined not only by their inherent economic or military assets but also by their potential role as the "core state" of a broader civilization-based coalition. Some "core states" seem obvious. As noted, Russia is the core of the Orthodox world, with some ecclesiastical dissent from other Orthodox churches. China heads the Sinic civilization, India the Hindu civilization, and Japan the Japanese counterpart. But what about the Muslim world? Does the role fall to a Sunni- or a Shiite-majority nation? Or to the nation that has the most Muslims living within its borders? Or to the most economically or militarily powerful? Or to a new caliphate, created as a successor to the role of the Ottoman state? Similar ambiguity also exists for the Latin American or African civilizations. And what about Western civilization? History is a story of conflict among potential core states, not of acquiescence to the leadership of a single nation to lead them all, even in the face of common threat. It does not stretch the imagination to suggest that there will be conflict among potential core states of the same civilization, and the creation of competing alliances of core and second-tier states, over who speaks and acts for the broader civilization.

That said, considerable power could also lie in the hands of non-state actors that claim to speak in the name of the broader civilization, especially if it appears that its core state is inadequate to the task. In today's world, that usually falls to terrorist or revolutionary groups whose actions are designed to gin up awareness and support for their cause and dramatically confront their cultural enemies.

Second, the shift to a culture-oriented identity will create the likelihood that traditional culture-defining entities will claim a greater role in shaping policy. Historically, that role has most often fallen to organized religion, although there may be serious divisions within equally legitimate claimants to the role. The Catholic-Protestant or the Sunni-Shiite distinctions remain relevant in today's world, as do more philosophical distinctions between conservative and liberal interpretations of secular cultures and the rapidly expanding "cultures wars" within many nations.

Third, to some extent, the work of international organizations and other multinational entities will be redefined in a culture-dominated world. Culture and civilizational affinity will play a greater role in shaping blocs and alliances, which would be more likely to form among like-minded nations. The role of existing blocs such as the Arab League or the Organization of American States would see an enhanced role, and others would likely form, as would trade patterns and other associations shaped by similar affinities.

Sources of Stability and Instability

Stability within civilization-defined alignments would depend upon the clarity and acceptance of the hierarchy among its members. Dominant core states would be essential, or at least agreement on some power-sharing arrangement. Agreement about who defines the culture and settles disputes among contending factions is also important. The special role of fault-line nations where the boundaries between *us* and *them* are right at the next border or cut through the nation itself must be recognized. Internal subgroup differences also must be resolved, especially over issues such as religion or ethnic identity, usually by power sharing or spheres-of-influence pacts.

Stability among different civilizations is much more difficult. Old nation-state rivalries will still apply, probably enhanced by the new sense of cultural differences. All of the conventional metrics by which national power is measured, and all of the conventional mechanisms of conflict avoidance or resolution will still be in play. But by definition, issues of cultural identity are deeply emotional and do not easily lend themselves to item-by-item compromise. While the notion of diplomacy still applies, its more contemporary state-to-state manifestations in balance of power systems, deterrence, or institutionalized rule-based mediation seem less applicable in a world of culture-to-culture confrontations. Civilization-based conflicts are more existential and fundamental, and therefore probably more difficult to prevent or solve. It must be remembered that the Treaty of Westphalia, still the most important diplomatic achievement in creating the international system, succeeded only because it convinced the warring Catholic and Protestant forces to step outside their culture and religion-centered frame of reference to create the idea of the modern nation-state in which everybody could play by the same rules. No small task, but one that may need to be equaled should the world become a clash of civilizations.

The impact of catastrophic events like wars, natural disasters, famines, or pandemics will depend upon whether the fault lines fall along existing cultural boundaries or cut across such distinctions. While broader cross-cultural responses may be difficult to achieve unless the problems are perceived as truly universal, action within a particular culturally defined community may be easier to achieve because of the stronger sense of community. But if the issue somehow internally divides a culture— various subcommunities are differently impacted, or nations competing for the status of the "core" of the cultural community disagree on a common response, for example—such challenges may compromise or divide a culture by introducing new fault lines within the community.

What Would a "Clash of Civilizations" World Look Like Today?

In today's world, fault lines defined by issues of identity and culture remain the demarcation points of continuing confrontations, copiously illustrated by the multiple ethnic and religious struggles tied to the breakup of Yugoslavia, the continuing struggles in Northern Ireland, the Sunni-Shiite divisions in the Muslim world, the growing clashes between Muslims, Hindus, and Buddhists in South Asia, and many more, each revealing flashpoints with broader regional and global implications. Most of these confrontations are examples of what Huntington calls "fault line conflicts," essentially localized struggles in which contiguous communities act out their grievances against each other. Nasty, brutish, but never short, they rarely resolve the local conflict that spawned them, much less have lasting impact on the global clash of civilizations that defines them.

As Huntington suggests, the clash of civilizations at the global level is most likely to occur in the form of wars between "core nations," with all of the ambiguity that implies if a single core nation does not exist. Conventional wisdom suggests that heading the list of possible confrontations are military clashes between China and the United States, or between Russia and the European Union, and the United States. Each confrontation is in many ways a replay of old Cold War–era face-offs, with the clash-of-civilizations component replacing older ideological fault lines. And each is a product of the complex interplay of geopolitics, economic competition, and cultural differences, not easily understood in terms of any of single factor to the exclusion of the others. Simply put, in the real world, it will be difficult to tell which of these factors is most important, just as we never really could tell during the Cold War whether Moscow or Beijing were motivated by ideological considerations or old-fashioned geopolitics. Whatever the combination, each motivation strengthens the other, deepening and intensifying the confrontation into an existential engagement, a life-and-death battle between *us* and *them*.

NOTES

1. Florian Coulmas, *Identity: A Very Short Introduction* (Oxford University Press, 2019); Jeffrey Kopstein, *Comparative Politics: Interests, Identities, and Institutions in a Changing Global Order* (Cambridge University Press, 2014); Elizabeth Schmermund, ed., *Identity Politics: Opposing Viewpoints* (Greenhaven Press, 2018); Francis Fukuyama, *The Demand for Dignity and the Politics of Resentment* (Farrar, Straus, and Giroux, 2018); and Gerhard Reese, Amir Rosenmann, and James Cameron, *The Psychology of Globalization: Identity, Ideology, and Action* (Academic Press, 2019).
2. *Merriam-Webster's Dictionary*, http://www.merriam-webster.com/dictionary/culture.
3. Samuel P. Huntington, *The Clash of Civilizations and the Remaking of the World Order* (Simon and Schuster, 1996), 207.
4. Francis Fukuyama, *The End of History and the Last Man* (Free Press, 1992).

5. Manfred B. Steger, *Globalization: A Very Short Introduction* (Oxford University Press, 2017); Joseph E. Stiglitz, *Globalization and Its Discontents Revisited* (Norton, 2017); Dani Rodrik, *The Globalization Paradox: Democracy and the Future of the World Economy* (Norton, 2012).

6. Reese et al., *The Psychology of Globalization*; Ethan Watters, *Crazy Like Us: The Globalization of the American Psyche* (Free Press, 2011); Robin Cohen, *The Global Diaspora* (Routledge, 2008); Gordon Mathews, *Global Culture / Individual Identity* (Routledge, 2000).

7. Benjamin Barber, *Jihad vs. McWorld: Terrorism's Challenge to Democracy* (Ballentine, 1996).

8. Saskia Sassen, *The Global City* (Princeton University Press, 2001).

9. Antje Wiener, *Contestation and Constitution of Norms in Global International Relations* (Cambridge University Press, 2018); Hevina S. Dashwood, *The Rise of Corporate Social Responsibility: Mining and the Spread of Global Norms* (Cambridge University Press, 2014); Noele Crossley, *Evaluating the Responsibility to Protect: Mass Atrocity Prevention as a Consolidating Norm in International Society* (Routledge, 2016).

10. G. J. Meyer, *A World Undone: The Story of the Great War, 1914—1918* (Bantam, 2007); Barbara W. Tuchman, *The Guns of August* (Presidio, 2004); Barbara W. Tuchman, *The Proud Tower: 1890–1914* (Random House, 1996).

11. Norman A. Graebner, *The Versailles Treaty and Its Legacy: The Failure of the Wilsonian Vision* (Cambridge University Press, 2014); David A. Andelman, *A Shattered Peace: Versailles 1919 and the Price We Pay Today* (Wiley, 2014).

12. John B. Judis, *The Populist Explosion: How the Great Recession Transformed American and European Politics* (Columbia Global Reports, 2016); Pippa Norris and Ronald Inglehart, *Cultural Backlash: Trump, Brexit, and Authoritarian Populism* (Columbia University Press, 2019); Rovica Kaltwasser et al., *The Oxford Handbook of Populism* (Oxford University Press, 2018).

13. Richard J. Krickus, *Showdown: The Lithuanian Rebellion and the Breakup of the Soviet Empire* (Patomic Books, 1997); Thomas Lane et al., *The Baltic States* (Routledge, 2002).

14. Daniel Stockemer, *The National Front in France: Continuity and Change under Jean-Marie Le Pen and Marine Le Pen* (Springer, 2017); Jocelyn Evans and Gilles Ivaldi, *The 2017 French Presidential Election: A Political Reformation?* (Palgrave Macmillan, 2017).

15. Stephen Wall, *A Stranger in Europe: Britain and the EU from Thatcher to Blair* (Oxford University Press, 2008); Kevin O'Rourke, *A Short History of Brexit* (Penguin UK, 2019); Geoffrey Evans and Anand Menon, *Brexit and British Politics* (Polity, 2017).

16. David Fromkin, *The Peace to End All Peace: The Fall of the Ottoman Empire and the Creation of the Modern Middle East* (Holt, 2009); Andrew Mango, *Ataturk: A Biography of the Founder of Modern Turkey* (Henry Abrams, 2002); and Charles King, *Midnight at the Pera Palace: The Birth of Modern Instanbul* (Norton, 2015).

17. Soner Cagaptay, *Erdogan's Empire: Turkey and the Politics of the Middle East* (I. B. Tauris, 2019).

18. Huntington, *The Clash of Civilizations*, 207.

5

The Ideology Paradigm

THE PARADIGM

Ideology plays an important role in shaping the international system, influencing the identity and goals of state and non-state actors and shaping their modus operandi on the international stage. Like the other paradigms, it sometimes becomes an important factor in who we are, where we are or should be headed, and how we can get there. At times, the world seems to have been shaped by fundamental and existential ideological conflict, as in the Cold War struggle between communism and capitalism. At other times, ideology seems to slip into the background, as in the immediate post–Cold War world, which briefly and optimistically celebrated the "end of history," the rise of globalization and economic interdependence, and the widespread acceptance of democracy as the desirable and probably inevitable form of government.

The optimism and self-assurance didn't last long. Ideology, like the other paradigms built around the nation-state, economics, and identity and culture, once again is at the core of conflicts in the modern world. Not in the same way or system-defining intensity that characterized its role in the Cold War, but in other ways, sometimes merging with other paradigms and sometimes redefining former struggles in terms more appropriate for the twenty-first century.

What is an ideology? There is no simple answer. Examples come to mind more easily than an all-encompassing definition: socialism, fascism, communism, capitalism, liberalism, and conservatism, making it tempting to say that ideologies are labeled with words that end in "ism." But does that mean that individualism, environmentalism, or feminism are also ideologies, at least in some sense? For our purposes, a more precise definition is needed, but one still flexible enough to allow for the diversity of what different ideologies tell us and how they are evoked in political discourse.[1]

The Oxford Dictionary defines ideology as "a system of ideas and ideals, especially one which forms the basis of economic or political theory and policy."[2] *Merriam-Webster's Dictionary* calls it a set of "integrated assertions, theories, and aims that constitute a sociopolitical program," adding later that it sometimes also is "a visionary theory."[3] Other definitions add words like "doctrines," "social movements," "myths and symbols," and "blueprints." Taken together, they collectively establish that ideologies are complex and multifaceted intellectual frameworks that explain and shape the world around us.

The ideology paradigm posits:

- **An ideological paradigm establishes a cognitive system that tells us what the world is like and how it works.**

It describes the world around us and how we fit into it. It gives us an intellectual frame of reference and tells us the identity and characteristics of the players in the international system. They can be conventional nation-states, economic or social classes, or others defined by ethnic or religious identities, each playing its role. Ideology also gives us a sense of the rules of engagement. The system can be defined in structural terms (a hegemonic or a multipolar configuration, for example) or in terms of the playbook that defines how it works (a balance of power or collective security system, for example). Ideology also tells us about the causal factors that animate the system. For Marxists, that reality is built around economic factors, the nature and ownership of what they call "the means of production," and how the class structure shapes society and the broader international system. Capitalists also acknowledge the centrality of economic factors and then build a different reality based on the importance of a free market and private ownership. Fascists, on the other hand, usually stress some sense of a mythically defined racial and ethnic identity, embodied in a charismatic leader and a mass movement and usually defined within the context of traditional social and political institutions. Populists focus on the central importance of the common people, whose identity and aspirations are embodied in a charismatic leader who defends them against self-serving domestic elites and "others" who have defiled the social unity of a once-united nation. More broadly, conservatives stress the importance of social continuity and the preservation of traditional cultural and political institutions, while liberals focus on the importance of change and "progressive" adaptation. And so it goes, with each ideology broadly setting the stage for the implementation of its beliefs and goals.

- **Ideologies establish a system of values and standards of behavior as guides to individual and collective action.**

In terms appropriate to their overall cognitive model, they tell us what is "good" and "bad" or "progressive" and "regressive." Sometimes the values are absolute, setting forth standards that are always appropriate (the sanctity of human life, human rights, or nonviolence, for example). And sometimes they are more relative or situational, telling us what's right or wrong in this particular moment in this particular situation (Marx's admonition to support the "progressive" forces of the moment in order to move the dialectical evolution of society forward toward a communist society, or the acceptability of creating tactical alliances with less-than-perfect allies for the sake of advancing a broader cause). At the operational level, such values provide us with the litmus tests that give at least some guidance for our day-to-day actions. In the real world, such judgments are often difficult and conflicted, subject to differing interpretations of the meaning of the original doctrine and of its interpretation in specific situations.

- **Ideologies set goals, sometimes in terms of creating utopian futures and sometimes more modestly in terms simply improving the nature of society.**

Utopias come in many forms. The most ambitious set high and sometimes distant goals, promising the attainment of a perfect world, ranging from the monarchist's notion of a stable social and political order built on the divine right of monarchs, Marx's notion of a communist future free of class struggle, or liberal democracy's model of a system based on the consent of the governed living in free and open societies. The less ambitious variations play a more modest but still important role, calling on us to constantly strive toward a better, if never quite perfect, order of things.

- **Ideologies frequently set forth guidance on how to navigate our way toward such better futures.**

Ideologies frequently, but not always, provide guidelines and strategic guidance on how we can accomplish their goals. Such road maps may be broadly drawn, giving us a general direction but not a detailed step-by-step plan of action. For Marxists, "class struggle" was the broadly defined strategy toward a communist future. But the nature of the class struggle had to be redefined at each stage of society's progress toward that future, giving rise to endless conflicts over the correct interpretation of the current stage and how best to move forward.

Some ideologies focus more on establishing the processes through which society and the international community determine their future. For them, the journey is more important than the goal. Western notions of democracy frequently stress issues, such as the creation of democratic institutions and their social and institutional prerequisites such as freedom of speech, wide-scale enfranchisement, the right of assembly, a free press, the rule of law, and other issues linked to the empowerment of the voters, rather than the specific content of the policies that result from democratic rule.

- **Ideologies frequently define the criteria for establishing the political legitimacy of a particular form of government, often focusing primarily on the process of choosing leaders rather than on the ultimate goals or short-term policies of the state.**

Legitimacy establishes the right of a particular leader or a form of government to exercise political power. It is the litmus test by which the leader—a monarch, president, prime minister, or authoritarian modernizer—proves his or her right to govern. For it to accomplish its intended task, it must also be widely accepted by those who will be governed. Like it or not, that person has a claim to the throne, the Oval Office in the White House, the president's office in the Kremlin's Senate Building, or wherever the seat of power may lie. That said, history teaches us that legitimacy can be challenged; the claimant is not the true heir to the throne, or the election was rigged, or, more ominously, the process of choice itself is flawed. On such dissent, elections are disputed and votes recounted, coups and counter-coups are staged, and revolutions are made.

Broadly speaking, legitimacy can be established in five ways, each with implications for the role that ideology might play.[4] The first and oldest is to establish legitimacy by some attribute of the leader. The usual criterion is bloodline, which underpins the notion that power is inherited through dynastic systems from generation to generation. Such thinking is deeply rooted in traditional monarchies and has pro forma survived into the modern era of constitutional monarchies.

Second, legitimacy may be conveyed by divine choice. The divine right of monarchs, especially when coupled with the notion of dynastic succession, became the de facto political ideology of the countless monarchies of Europe well into the twentieth century. But the idea was not unique to Europe. Chinese emperors were sustained by "the mandate of heaven," the withdrawal of which could be signaled through defeat on the battlefield or widespread natural disasters.

Third, legitimacy also can be conveyed by the mastery of the nuances of the ideology itself, creating a sort of ideological priesthood whose interpretations of the doctrine conveyed some measure of legitimacy to the regime and to its leadership. Communist regimes in the Soviet Union and Eastern Europe attached great importance to the "correct" interpretation of the doctrine, frequently stoking arcane debates among the theoreticians and conflict with other communist regimes.

Fourth, ideologies also can be used to argue that the regime has some special, ideologically ordained role to play in building the future. The authoritarian Leninist model adopted in various forms by revolutionary movements in Russia and China was kept in place long after the revolution because it allegedly was the best way to rapidly industrialize backward nations. The same logic is offered by many of today's authoritarian modernizers who are faced with the same task; whatever the nuances of their particular situation, they argue that the creation of modern industrial societies, a central feature to their program as transformational leaders, requires continued discipline and centralized leadership.

Fifth, and most important in the modern world, legitimacy is conveyed by the process by which leaders are chosen. Primary emphasis falls on satisfying the procedural requirements rather than on any of the other attributes of legitimacy. It's a game of numbers, but not always of simple majorities. In a single-member, first-past-the-post plurality system, that means you don't need a majority, just one more vote than anybody else. But in other systems that require a majority, a runoff election between the top two vote recipients may be necessary. A system based on proportional representation plays by different rules, allocating the seats among the parties in accordance with their share of the vote. There are seemingly endless and nuanced variations on how the system may be fine-tuned, to say nothing of the impact of special institutional arrangements such as the U.S. Electoral College.

The important point is that legitimacy is conveyed by the system's faith in a process, not the characteristics or qualifications of the candidates or the ideologically acceptable content of the policies they will pursue. Win the game, and win power and legitimacy. It is the logical and inevitable extension of the underlying principles of democratic rule. In the modern world, it has de facto become an ideology in its own right, a goal, if not a utopia, to be pursued for its own intrinsic good. Woodrow Wilson argued at the Versailles Conference at the end of World War I that creating democracies to replace the vanquished autocracies of Europe would contribute to establishing peace on the continent, and a host of later American presidents from Franklin D. Roosevelt to George W. Bush have pursued similar policies of democratization through "regime change" and "nation building" to advance the concept of democratic rule, assuming that it would make a difference in how the world worked.

Two caveats must be noted about the nature of the ideologies that flesh out this paradigm. First, as with the other paradigms, it is not unusual that the ideological paradigm will merge with other paradigms to provide a more nuanced view of the world. The nation-state and the ideology paradigms make comfortable bedfellows, giving us the notions of national-socialism, the doctrine of Nazi Germany, or socialism in one country, Stalin's version of defensive Russian nationalism combined with the developmental strategy for the industrialization of a still backward nation. Other examples abound, from Islamic democracy to Xi Jinping's "socialism with Chinese characteristics."

Second, not all elements of an ideological paradigm may be equally important at the same time. Revolutionary and transformational doctrines may go through a series of stages, first stressing the revolutionary aspects of the ideology and later shifting focus to the elements that focus on building and governing the newly created regime. Lenin's doctrine of revolutionary action yielded to Stalin's nation-building strategies embodied in the five-year plans and "socialism in one country." Eventually they were followed by Nikita Khrushchev's ideas of the "full flowering of socialism" and Leonid Brezhnev's doctrine of "developed socialism," a

1970s Marxist equivalent of Western notions of postindustrial society. Each was the logical (or perhaps politically necessary) next stage on the road to the ever-receding goal of full communism, and each provided the current view of how far we've come, where we next need to go, and, most importantly, the reassurance that the current leadership had things under control.

THE POSSIBLE FUTURES

When viewed from the perspective of the ideological paradigm, several possible alternative futures emerge (see table 5.1). They include:

- **A universalistic and humanistic ideology emerges**, built around universalism, humanism, economic and political empowerment, democratic rule, and social responsibility, merging with an emerging global culture,

- **Ideological conflict reemerges**, stoking old or redefining new philosophical, political, economic, and social divisions, offering new definitions of "left" and "right" and potentially changing the alignment of political forces and formal institutions; renewed ideological conflict may focus on "process ideologies" that

Table 5.1. The Ideology Paradigm

Global Humanistic Ideology	Ideological Conflict Reemerges	National Ideology	Populism
Global norms stress humanitarianism, empowerment, and democracy	Conflict reemerges between "new" right and left and over issues of political legitimacy	Ideologically defined nation-states disrupt the international system	Nation transformed by populist ideology, which fuses economic and cultural nationalism with class struggle

Table 5.1 (*cont.*)

Global Humanistic Ideology	Ideological Conflict Reemerges	National Ideology	Populism
Sovereignty gradually yields to international institutions	Redefined ideological conflicts occur within and among states	Such nation-states frequently create authoritarian single-party regimes	Charismatic leaders emerge, drawing support from disaffected or marginal elements
Emphasis placed on conflict mediation, R2P, and transnational issues like global warming	Formal institutions are transformed and repurposed by new ideological struggles	The nation and the party are led by charismatic authoritarian figures, frequently espousing a transformational doctrine	Political disputes framed in terms of restoring past achievements lost to weakness or betrayal
International civil society grows in salience and effectiveness	Ideological conflicts lead to "tribalism" and hyper-partisanship	The party and the state penetrate and control all aspects of society	Populist nations usually seek to redefine the nation's role in the international system
Global ideology supports reassessment of in-group and out-group identities	New interpretations of democracy and legitimacy challenge classic "liberal" and pluralistic views	Such nations frequently become revisionist and revolutionary states	Scapegoats, both at home and abroad, are blamed for the nation's problems

determine the legitimacy of how leaders and governments are chosen rather than on the content of public policy,

- A "national ideology" becomes the dominant fusion of national identity and ideology, merging distinctive national and cultural identities with right- or left-wing ideologies to create idiosyncratic and allegedly superior belief systems, frequently associated with a sense of exceptionalism and manifest destiny; in its most extreme form it could create transformational and chiliastic regimes reminiscent of the Cold War.

- Populism emerges as an alternative to conventionally institutionalized political action, shifting the focus of political divisions to elite-mass distinctions, conveying power to charismatic leaders and mass movements, and redefining the role of existing political parties and formal institutions.

A UNIVERSALISTIC AND HUMANISTIC IDEOLOGY EMERGES

While having much in common with the earlier notion of an emerging global culture, a universalistic and humanistic ideology requires the development of a more distinct frame of reference setting forward the basic principles of the belief system; a clearer sense of how the ideology is linked to political, social, and economic change in the real world; an examination of how the doctrine would transform the international system; and a clearer notion of what such a brave new world would look like in the future. Elements of the doctrine would overlap with and be influenced by other paradigms; continuing emphasis on the nation-state and/or identity and culture paradigms would weaken its commitment to greater universalism, while emphasis on the paradigms of economic, social, or cultural globalization would strengthen its universalistic relevance and appeal.[5]

Following are some key concepts at the core of the doctrine.

Universalism, which stresses the universal validity of core values and beliefs and a commitment to common social norms. Emphasis falls on a commitment to a cosmopolitan perspective that all humans belong to a single global community defined by a sense of common membership, shared norms of private and public actions that define a sense of common morality, and a commitment to work within common economic and political institutions that embody this sense of universal identity.

Humanitarianism, which further emphasizes the sense of common communal identity and the promotion of human material, social, and spiritual well-being. It may be embodied in either secular humanitarianism, deemphasizing the role of religion, or ecumenical humanitarianism, which combines religion with a broader sense of common human values that transcend specific institutionalized faiths.

Empowerment and democratic rule, which emphasize direct personal and institutional involvement in important political, economic, and social processes, going beyond a sense of formal enfranchisement to promote a strong sense of agency and direct action undertaken through democratic institutions sustained by free competitive elections, civil rights, free media, and an active and pluralistic civil society.

Equality, which is closely linked with the sense of membership in a common international community and the growing empowerment of its equal members, impacting the doctrine at two levels. The first deals with equal access to and participation within political, social, and economic institutions; everybody gets to vote, at least in terms of formal enfranchisement, and everybody has access to participation through other mechanisms such as direct action, interests groups, political parties, and the like. In Orwell's terms, "all animals are equal," or at least as equal as possible in the real world. The second sense of equality is more controversial in both theory and practice. It describes a sense of greater equality in terms of broader criteria such as wealth, influence, social standing, and access to public and private services and institutions such as education or employment, and the like, and implies a process of leveling-up or leveling-down to achieve such equity. To alter the second half of Orwell's dictum from *Animal Farm*, "and some will never be more or less equal than others."

Social responsibility, which establishes an expanding sense of communal responsibility to take direct action to implement and defend the values set forth by the doctrine. It was first embodied in formal documents such as the UN Universal Declaration of Human Rights, adopted in 1948 by the General Assembly, and a host of later enactments covering the rights of children and women, or other issues, and subsequently expanded by the R2P doctrine, endorsed by all UN member states in 2005, which called upon all nations to take action against genocide, war crimes, ethnic cleansing, and crimes against humanity. Similar norms or treaties create a moral imperative that the international community respond to the impact of mass migration, natural disasters, and other events that require coordinated international action. While the record of success is mixed at best, the sense of a moral imperative to assume joint responsibility has been established and a rudimentary institutional framework created.

The Structure of the Universalistic and Humanistic Ideology Paradigm

The initial impact of a universalistic and humanistic ideology will vary from state to state, depending on the nature of the dominant paradigm before the transformation begins. For most traditionally defined nation-states, the process of change will be gradual as the notions of sovereignty, national identity, and territorial integrity are reinterpreted in light of the growing acceptance of universalistic and humanistic norms. It will begin with the transformation of public and private values and norms, broadening the acceptance of international and transnational perspectives and the assumption of broader responsibilities. Nation-states and international institutions will be transformed from the inside out. Formal institutional change will come later, as the institutions are repurposed and reconfigured as universalistic and humanitarian values reshape their commitment to the international community.

If the economic or culture and identity paradigms are initially dominant, the transformation will take a slightly different course. Prior acceptance of economic globalization and interdependence will facilitate the acceptance of a similarly universalistic ideological perspective. Conversely, continued emphasis on national or regional economic priorities will complicate the transition, perhaps leaving islands of resistance and standalone exceptionalism defiantly operating outside, but perhaps not in direct opposition to, a growing sense of internationalism. The same would be true of the impact of identity and culture. Acceptance of a sense of transnational or global cultural identity will facilitate the emergence of universalistic and humanistic perspectives and norms, while resistance based on a lingering sense of a distinct identity and culture would delay or compromise the transformation.

That said, the important point is that the overall impact of a universalistic and humanistic ideology would be to reduce the level of international conflict and facilitate conflict avoidance, mediation, and other forms of peacekeeping. In institutional terms, its impact would be manifested through the transformation of the traditional nation-state through its implementation of broader universalistic and humanistic goals; through existing international institutions such as the United Nations and its many subordinate economic, social, and humanitarian entities such as the World Health Organization, UNESCO (United Nations Educational, Scientific, and Cultural Organization), or the International Labor Organization, to name a few; through an expanding assortment of international and regional economic actors in the private and public sectors such as multinational corporations and regulatory agencies such as the European Agency for Safety and Health at Work, the European Environmental Agency, the European Center for Disease Prevention and Control, and through counterpart bodies in other regions; and through an expanding and increasingly invasive assortment of international civil society agencies such as the Red Cross, the Red Crescent, OXFAM (the Oxford Committee on Famine Relief), or Doctors Without Borders.

How Power Is Distributed

While the formal institutions of government, the private sector, and civil society ultimately will be transformed by the emergence of a universalistic and humanistic ideology, it is important to realize that the process of change will begin with the gradual reinterpretation and repurposing of the formal structures as we now know them. The nation-state, for example, will gradually become less preoccupied with the formal attributes of sovereignty, territorial integrity, and national power and more concerned with using the mechanisms of the state to implement the broader global agenda rooted in the new doctrine. The notion of the "national interest" will be broadened and reinterpreted, as will the sense of responsibility for the collateral costs of actions that transcend traditional national boundaries. To be sure, the de jure realities of much of the Westphalian world will remain. Technically nation-states will retain the legal right to invoke sovereignty in most cases, but they will voluntarily choose not to use it in the interest of implementing commonly accepted policies and norms. Conversely, technically non-sovereign entities such as international organizations or international civil society will acquire greater de facto authority, a consequence of the acceptance of common norms and the de facto reluctance of nation-states to exercise their powers to the fullest extent. There will be limits and exceptions, of course. Some nation-states will more jealously guard their prerogatives than others. And the ebb and flow of domestic politics also will establish parameters, sometimes requiring a narrower interpretation of the nation's willingness to cooperate and sometimes extending such cooperation to new levels.

Increasing influence also will accrue to those actors who are traditionally seen as the sources and interpreters of social norms and values. International or regional organizations will play a greater role, with bodies such as the United Nations General Assembly or the EU Parliament, Council, and Commission serving as the agenda setters and advocates of more extensive international efforts. International courts such as the United Nation's International Court of Justice, the International Criminal Court, EU Court of Justice or Court of Human Rights will play a more direct role, as will other regional bodies such as the Inter-American Court of Human Rights or the African Court of Justice. Respected nations individually may also be involved, especially if their "soft power" ratings win the respect of others. Organized religious bodies will be important, especially to the extent that an ecumenical sense of common purpose overcomes sectarian differences. In the private sector, socially responsible multinational corporations and trade associations will play a similar role. The media will be important interpreters and disseminators of a broader sense of commitment and action, as will educational and cultural institutions and the always chattering class of "public intellectuals" who populate the media on a global scale. Entertainers, too, will sometimes be directly involved, propagating the broader sense of commitment or supporting efforts to raise money for relief efforts in specific cases such as the Concert for Bangladesh (1971), the No Nucs Concerts (1979), and the Live Earth Concert (2007), to name a few of many similar events.[6]

Sources of Stability and Instability

The most important source of stability will lie in the depth and scope of the international commitment to the common values embodied in a universalistic and humanistic perspective. Such commitment will initially grow slowly, spurred on by its apparent success in mitigating conflict and the degree to which increasing institutionalization and acceptance by civil society create a sense of inertia and inevitability. There will be a tipping point, or more likely several different tipping points for different audiences, beyond which the validity of the doctrine is accepted as conventional wisdom.

On the other hand, however, a commitment to a universalistic and humanitarian ideology will be compromised by the perception that it fails to meet the challenges of an increasingly complex world. It looked good in theory, but we just couldn't make it work in the real world. Performance legitimacy is essential; perceived failure to deal with real-world problems and conflicts will undercut its acceptance and slow or reverse its support. Intensifying economic and cultural conflicts will have a similar impact, especially if they are linked to growing "my country first" populist movements and reduced involvement with existing international bodies. As before, there would be a tipping point where previous commitments would be revised or abandoned. Especially important would be the abandonment of key elements of this perspective by one or more significant world power, as with the American withdrawal from the Paris Agreement on climate change and global warming.

Unexpected crises or catastrophic shocks to the system could cut either way. On the one hand, they could result in the emergence of a heretofore unseen level of a truly global response, informed by a deepening universal and humanistic ideology and implemented through increasing reliance on more aggressive and proactive responses from existing global or regional bodies like the United Nations or various regional blocs and an increased role for international civil society. If the problem were perceived as truly global—*global* warming and environmental deterioration, or a devastating *pan*demic, or something of the sort—it might produce one of those seminal moments in which paradigms change across the board in response to an unavoidable confrontation with reality. Such unusually rapid change would be reinforced by the presence of a sense of global culture and identity and a deepening of a truly global economy.

But it could also go the other way, undercutting whatever sense of a universalistic and humanistic ideology existed and replacing it with more parochial frames of reference that stress divisive national, cultural, or economic identities. When we needed it most, our commitment to a universalistic and humanistic ideology failed to produce common action in the face of catastrophic challenges, and in desperation we defaulted to older and more parochial frames of reference, as nation-states, cultures, or economic classes. Previous momentum toward a more universalistic ideological perspective would be eroded or possibly destroyed, and once-supportive notions such as economic globalization or the creation of a global cultural and identity would suffer a similar fate.

What Would a World of a Universalistic and Humanistic Ideology Look Like?

A world of a universalistic and humanistic ideology would look a bit utopian, and would probably be unreachable in its purist form. It seems to run contrary to all of our attempts to identity ourselves as nation-states, distinct cultures, or separate economic systems throughout most of our history. Yet even from this broader perspective, the search for answers to recurring problems has repeatedly compelled us to envision solutions on an ever-widening scale. The search for security expanded from the fate of the individual nation-state to alliance systems, then to the balance of power, and then to ever-larger collective security schemes embodied in the League of Nations and the United Nations, each imperfect in its own way but collectively a confirmation of a willingness to look for broader answers to bigger problems. Growing economic interdependence, whether celebrated or lamented, has also brought us closer to looking at the world in similar ways, as have the technologies of travel and communication and the creation of an increasingly global culture.

IDEOLOGICAL CONFLICT REEMERGES

Ideological conflict reemerges as a primary source of division in the international system, producing new self-perceptions and institutional alignments that animate philosophical, economic, and social conflict both within nation-states and the international system. Most likely associated with redefinitions of the older concepts of "left" and "right" or with redefining the meaning of political legitimacy, these divisions create new fault lines and raise fundamental questions about the structure and modus operandi of political life at all levels. Sometimes they will bring about new meanings and political alignments under old labels, most likely as the traditional "left" and "right" try to redefine themselves and regroup in light of new political realities. At other times, new ideological variations emerge as national identity and ideology merge to create national variations of broader ideological themes, labeled "national ideology" below. In other cases, older ideological and political conflicts will be recast under the broader mantle of left- or right-wing populism, which reconceptualizes social conflicts in terms of more generic elite-mass distinctions. This variation also is considered separately, labeled "populism" below.

The "New Left" and the "New Right"

The "new left" and the "new right" have their origins in more conventional ideological points of view, initially deemphasized by the briefly held "end of history" argument after the Cold War and politically embodied in the "third way" centrist administrations of American president Bill Clinton and British prime minister Tony Blair, both of whom, however briefly, moved their nations toward a commonly accepted political "center." Both drew added legitimacy through the widespread and initially uncritical acceptance of globalization in the 1980s and 1990s, until its growing economic and political implications produced growing opposition after the 2008 global economic crisis. For the "new left," such opposition was seen in the revival of hardcore issues such as the growing concentration of wealth in fewer and fewer hands, the stagnation of workers' wages and standard of living, and in the hollowing out of the traditional blue-collar working and middle classes. The "old left" failed to respond effectively to these challenges. The British Labour Party, the French Socialist Party, and the American Democratic Party all lost support, challenged by emerging populist movements or by leftist challengers such as Jeremy Corbin in the Labour Party and more radical elements within the Democratic Party like Bernie Sanders, whose platform in the run-up to the 2020 presidential election tried to move the party substantially to the left.[7]

The "new left" also drew added support from the increasing acceptance of broader social and lifestyle issues such as diversity, inclusion, empowerment, and the acceptance of same-sex marriages and gender-identity issues. Once-shunned third-rail issues carefully avoided by mainstream politicians took center stage, greeted by increasing acceptance by center-left politicians and parties and by broad support among certain sections of the voting public.

The "new right" also responded to many of the same issues, sometimes focusing on more traditional responses such as the defense of institutional stability, market-based capitalism, the important role of entrepreneurs and "job creators," globalization and free trade, and the defense of traditional privilege and elite status. In foreign policy, the response usually stressed greater reliance on traditional nation-states as the key actors, the defense of national sovereignty, and greater reliance on military and economic strength. The right-wing version of populism morphed into an appeal to displaced or marginalized victims of globalization and automation, the traditional middle class that feared it no longer was the bedrock of a once-stable society, and those concerned with profound changes in culture and social norms. Racial and ethnic overtones soon emerged, pitting rural small towns and rust-belt regions against their increasingly urbanized, ethnically and racially diverse, younger, better educated, and more tolerant counterparts.

Legitimacy and "Process Ideologies"

Yet another resurgence of ideological struggle is linked to the increasing importance of what we call "process" or "instrumental" ideologies, which deal with the *processes* rather than the *outcomes* of political action. While most ideologies prioritize the substantive dimensions of the doctrine—the kind of society that will emerge—process ideologies focus primarily on how political institutions establish legitimacy. It's not about the goals. It's about the rules of the game and the playbooks that govern the day-to-day ebb and flow of political life. The traditional variations include descriptions like "monarchy," "aristocracy," "theocracy," or "democracy." The most important elements in defining the system attach to how the leaders are chosen, about what conveys legal and broader societal legitimacy, and how elites and the general public interact in the game of politics. Once we agree on *how and by whom* political decisions should be made, the question of what policies they decide to follow becomes far less relevant, at least in philosophical terms. *They*, whoever *they* are, have been granted the right to rule over us—by divine right in a monarchy, by social position and probably wealth in an aristocracy, by their role as spokespersons of the god(s) in a theocracy, and by us, the people, in a democracy. We may or may not like the policies they choose, and ultimately—but probably not until the next election—we can cast them aside and choose new leaders. But if we have accepted the core definition of legitimacy and the rules of the game that they establish, we have de facto also accepted the parameters within which change can occur. Sometimes—especially in a democracy—we elevate that definition of legitimacy to the most important element of how politics should work. To be sure, other elements will also be present, but for some reason, we have chosen to emphasize *process* over *outcome*.

The Structure of New Ideological Conflict

For the most part, the initial phases of new ideological conflict play out within the framework of the old structures. The nation-state as we know it remains, but internally transformed by the substance and tactics of the new fault lines. At first, the structure of the international system will see little institutional change. But the ways in which the nation-state and the international order operate will change. A "new normal" will replace the "old normal," signaling significant changes in the playbook that governs day-to-day politics. Ideological conflict within nations will eventually realign their priorities and roles within the international system. Nations once committed to an activist role in promoting a stable international system may turn inward, placing their own priorities ahead of further international involvement. Nations once focused on their own economic and social development may begin to play a more expansive role as the newly emergent major powers of the day. Commitment to an expanding role for international organizations and humanitarian or peacekeeping interventionist policies may yield to new priorities based on self-interest, nonintervention, and withdrawal.

Two political battles will occur at the same time, each affecting the style and outcome of the other. The first will be within conflicting ideological positions and what they imply for the nation's role in the world. The "new left" and the "old left" will have to work out their internal differences on how the nation will fit into the international system. What are our goals? Who are our allies and enemies? And how do we engage this reconceptualized world? The same struggle will occur on the right, as the "new right" and the "old right" fight it out. Much is at stake: control over a reunified or irrevocably split constituency; the capture and redefinition of time-honored political symbols and icons; the control over political parties and their organizational and financial apparatus; and the loyalty and votes of old or new constituents. Existing political parties will be internally transformed or cast aside. New parties or leader-centered movements will emerge, some hoping to rebuild "big tent" organizations that draw support from many constituencies, and others creating more narrowly based or single-issue parties to appeal to clearly defined and highly motivated supporters.

The second battle will be between whatever emerges to claim the mantle of "left" or "right," each probably still internally divided over the nuances of the doctrine and the details of policy. As with virtually all ideological struggles, conflicting interpretations will remain, each shaping the conflicts within nations and the alignments within the international system.

How Power Is Distributed

The reemergence of ideologically based alignments creates an unstable mix in which power is shaped by constantly changing factors, including changes in existing formal institutions, altered or repurposed by the emergence of redefined core beliefs and a new playbook; conflict among new and older but reconfigured political parties and movements, reflecting the underlying ideological struggles of the day; changes within the institutional context of increasingly powerful and emboldened executive leadership, often placed in the hands of charismatic and untraditional presidents or prime ministers who have captured more traditional parties or built a personal following that cuts across traditional constituencies; increasing polarization of political conflict, a consequence of an as yet unresolved ideological struggle and the increase disfunction of formal institutions and political parties; and last, but increasingly important, a changing political battlefield shaped by the impact of new communications technologies that affect public opinion and mobilize voters.

In short, it's a new and complex game, played better by some than others. Some political truths remain constant. First, fortune favors the bold; innovative leaders who can create new issues or redefine old ones acquire a tactical advantage, at least at first. So-called wedge issues that divide once stable constituencies and regroup their members into new identities and alliances play a significant role in defining the "new normal" and the meaning of "left" and "right."

Sources of Stability and Instability

While initially the impact of the revival of ideological conflict between the "new left" and the "new right" will be felt within nation-states, ultimately it will spill over into the international community as new domestic political realities redefine foreign policy priorities and alliance structures. What happens at home doesn't stay at home. Long-standing friendships will cool and new antagonisms emerge, and former enemies will become today's allies or partners of convenience.

Institutional adaptability will be of key importance in maintaining stability during ideological realignment. The formal institutions of nation-states and the international system will have to alter or reinterpret the rules of the game and adjust to the "new normal." The mechanisms of civil society—political parties, lobbies and interest groups, the media, and the myriad assortment of actors involved in political life—will face similar adjustments. Quick and artful adjustment will facilitate the transition and help to legitimate whatever new realities and relationships emerge, while dogged and uncompromising resistance will prolong and encumber the transition. Worse yet, continuing and deeply rooted ideological conflict will lock both nation-states and the international system into prolonged and seemingly irresolvable polarization and institutional gridlock, a fate not unlike the earliest and most perilous years of the Cold War.

Catastrophic challenges will impact in different ways. Natural disasters, widespread migrations caused by manmade or natural events, or other shocks to the system may or may not acquire ideological significance. Global warming, environmental degradation, mass migrations, or pandemics can easily morph into ideologically significant issues, variously interpreted from a right- or left-wing perspective. More importantly, they can easily be turned into controversial wedge issues used by skilled politicians to shift the nature of the political debate. Global warming and climate change, for example, have acquired a political life of their own independent of the merits of scientific discourse, as more recently has the nature of and response to the COVID-19 pandemic.

Catastrophic events also impact what we have termed "process ideologies," which provide a sense of legitimacy for the manner in which political choices are made. In the simplest sense, the basic rule of "performance legitimacy" applies: if the way in which we choose to govern ourselves doesn't provide answers to the problems we face, we need to reexamine our institutional choices. Sometimes the problem may just be the leaders we have chosen, so the answer is to choose different leaders. But what if the problems persist and we begin to question the validity of the fundamental institutions? Perhaps a monarchy fails to prove a workable government capable of meeting our everyday needs, much less the occasional crises? Or a single-party regime led by an authoritarian modernizer? Or a democracy? While performance legitimacy is usually based on an assessment of a government's success or failure over time, dramatic failure to deal with a single catastrophic challenge may provide the final straw that tips the balance and spawns revolutionary change.

What Would an Ideologically Redefined World Look Like?

The first stage of such a realignment would look very much like today's world. In the United States, the "new" and "old" left are in as yet unresolved conflict over the economic and social meaning of each variation. The American right evidences similar disunion; the "old," or traditionally conservative right is locked in battle with the "new" increasingly populist right. Ideological polarization within and between parties and institutional gridlock in the legislative and executive branches have brought business as usual to a halt. In Great Britain, Brexit initially divided the Conservative Party, leading to the resignations of two prime inisters, David Cameron and Theresa May, and the eventual emergence of Boris Johnson, who supported British withdrawal from the EU and successfully led the Tories to victory in the 2019 election. Following the election, the Labour Party fell into disarray with the resignation of Jeremy Corbin after the party's poor showing in the polls, eventually choosing the more moderate Keir Starmer to try to pick up the pieces.[8] The 2017 French presidential election produced a runoff in which neither of the second-round candidates represented the traditionally center-right Gaullist coalition, now labeled the Republicans, or the Socialist Party, both of which were increasingly rejected by voters. The final contenders were Emmanuel Macron, a candidate of the self-styled En Marche party, and Marine Le Pen, who headed the far-right National Front, now renamed the National Rally. Macron easily won, and En Marche was swept into power in the legislature in June 2017, completely reshaping French politics in ways not seen since the election of Valery Giscard d'Estaing in 1974.[9] "New left" or "new right" socialist or populist governments also came to power in Greece, Italy, and Hungary. German stability, once reassuringly manifested in the grand coalitions formed by the center-right Christian Democrats and the center-left Social Democrats when no single-party majority emerged, now seems open to doubt, especially with the coming departure of Angela Merkel and the emergence of the Alternative for Germany (AfD), a right-wing populist party.[10]

The long-term impact of these nascent realignments is far from clear. It is likely that other nations will engage in similar moments of soul searching and uncertainty. What seems unchallengeable is that ideology will play an increasingly important role in shaping their identity and role in a changing international system.

"NATIONAL IDEOLOGY" BECOMES THE DOMINANT FUSION OF NATIONAL IDENTITY AND IDEOLOGY

A "national ideology" emerges as a synthesis of an ideological paradigm with a national or cultural paradigm that establishes a unique and idiosyncratic hybrid identity appropriate for a particular nation-state or culture. It's a "we're different" argument, requiring a special adaptation of a more generic ideology to reflect our special needs or aspirations. It establishes a symbiotic relationship between the two halves of the doctrine. National or cultural identity roots it deeply into the existing world of conventional thinking, defined in already accepted terms of nation-states or broader cultural identities. Ideological identity defines it in broader terms, frequently setting it apart from similar but more conventional national or cultural iterations by establishing a sense of exceptionalism. The relationship between the two halves is symbiotic; each needs the other to complete the sense of special identity and mission. National or cultural identity alone is old news, the established conventional wisdom that, while still significant, has defined us ever since it emerged with the birth of the nation-state. Ideological identity and purpose, especially if linked to a transformational program that redefines the nation and its place in the world, animate and give direction to the new hybrid point of view. It matters little which comes first, whether an established nation-state or culture acquires a new sense of ideological purpose, or whether an established ideology finds a new home as a unique variation appropriate for a particular nation-state. The result is the same. Each renews, animates, and emboldens the other.

A national ideology goes beyond populism in two significant ways. First, its concept of communal or national identity is more strongly rooted in the creation of a dominant and usually aggressive nation-state destined to transform the world; we're not only different by virtue of our unique national or cultural identity and our idiosyncratic interpretation of an already existing ideology, but we're also on a mission to transform the world in its image. It reinforces a sense of special ascriptive identity and community, uniquely vested in a traditionally defined nation-state (or in the aspiration to create one that does not yet exist) or in a sense of cultural identity that establishes a unique community. "We" aren't like anybody else, by virtue of history or cultural development, and therefore "we" must create our own variation of broader ideologically inspired identity. Sometimes it's also vested in a unique sense of destiny and the future; "we" are destined to build our own future world and to follow our special path to that end. The combinations span the gamut of ideological and national/cultural identities, from variations such as Arab socialism and Islamic democracy, Joseph Stalin's socialism in one country or Leonid Brezhnev's ideas of developed socialism, to the endless iterations of Mao Zedong thought, Deng Xiaoping thought, and the latest, Xi Jinping thought, to name but a few.

Second, the successful implementation of our national and ideological mission requires the creation of a proactive nation-state, a new form of political, economic, and social organization guided by the newly emergent doctrine but institutionalized through the creation of an all-power political entity that deeply penetrates and controls all phases of the lives of its citizens. Some will call it "totalitarianism" because of its all-encompassing need to control all aspects of life, while others will focus on the nuts-and-bolts description of the mechanism of a "party-state" or "Leninist" model in which a single centralized and all-powerful political party, guided and legitimated by its interpretation of the doctrine, takes control of all aspects of political, economic, and social activity. Whatever the terminology, the central reality remains the same: the nation, the doctrine, and the central apparatus of political, economic, and social control merge into the hands of a single elite.

The Structure of a National Ideology State

Typically, a national ideology state is built around an authoritarian merger of an already existing nation-state with a transformational ideology. Such regimes frequently begin as political movements initially built around fringe doctrines that purport to offer a "new" and frequently utopian and chiliastic view of the nation's transformation. Often they are rooted in some version of industrialization and economic modernization promising to drag a still-backward nation rapidly into the ranks of the advanced powers of the day. Closely linked to wide-ranging cultural and social transformations, they promise the creation of a "new" order of things and a "new" citizenry to populate and lead the transformation. In other cases, they are rooted in a promise to restore an idealized version of the nation's past cultural and political dominance. Mussolini promised to restore the glory of the Roman Empire, and the nineteenth-century Russian Slavophiles sought to reestablish a sense of a "pure" national identity rooted in Russian Orthodoxy, unquestioned obedience to an all-powerful tsar, and the central role of the preindustrial peasant culture as the true essence of Russia and its only hope for the future. Different iterations of a national ideology may be linked to either traditional right- or left-wing philosophies, sometimes combining elements of both to attract broader support. Such doctrines may be offered as a response to a national setback or tragedy—the loss of a war, the gradual decline of a once-powerful nation, or a stalled revolution whose utopian hopes and promises have failed to materialize. Or they may emerge as a series of progressive iterations on a common theme, each identified with a new leader who must put forward his or her updated version of an older truth in order to establish personal legitimacy.

Most national ideology states of the twentieth century fit the pattern. Both German national-socialism and Italian fascism were unique combinations of national themes with broader economic and social doctrines based on socialist, populist, or syndicalist thought, although both easily cooperated with more traditional right-wing business and commercial interests. The Russian revolution of 1917 and the Chinese revolution of 1911 both sought to transform their nations in economic, social, and political terms and were inspired by a sense of national weakness or failure and modeled after doctrines largely imported from the West. Their subsequent development, from Lenin's theory of a revolutionary vanguard and the dictatorship of the proletariat through to Putin's notions of "sovereign democracy" or Mao's doctrine of peasant revolution and the Great Leap Forward through to the economic and political implications of "Xi Jinping thought" and "socialism with Chinese characteristics," are typical of such hybrid doctrines. All reflect a common and evolving trajectory combining idiosyncratic national features with broader and frequently foreign-born doctrines.

How Power Is Distributed in a National Ideology State

National ideology regimes are typically built around the merger of the traditional nation-state and a single dominant political party that led the revolution against the old order and then transformed itself into an institutionalized governing elite worthy of today's label of a "deep state." Termed the "party-state" or the "Leninist model," it embodies the transformational zeal and single-minded purpose of a revolutionary movement with the bureaucratic apparatus of the state. In the early stages of the transformation, the "party-" or movement-centered half prevails, drawing together a disciplined cadre of party faithful, and eventually coalescing around a single doctrine and leader. Each in his own way, Benito Mussolini, Adolf Hitler, Vladimir Lenin, Joseph Stalin, and Mao Zedong all fit the model, as did the fascist, national-socialist, Bolshevik, or peasant-backed communist movements they led. Power was divided among various leadership or ideological factions, and conflict was endemic and frequently deadly.

While eventual victory ends some forms of internal conflict—sometimes only after a prolonged and deadly purge of the party or movement itself—it brings new divisions and alignments. The party, which had been the leading core of the broader movement, expands its jurisdiction over the more traditional apparatus of the state bureaucracy, turning it to its new purpose, purging its less-than-enthusiastic survivors, and, most insidiously, learning how to control its every thought and action. Stalin's assumption of control after Lenin's death in 1924 became the model if not the day-to-day blueprint for others. First he took control of the Communist Party, purging the Bolshevik old guard and any hint of remaining opposition, and then manipulated the party apparatus through his power as party general secretary to place his supporters in controlling positions in all aspects of public life. He finished the job in the late 1930s through the deadly purges. Equally important was the changing role of the party apparatus itself. From a small band of revolutionaries before 1917, it was transformed into a controlling bureaucracy at the core of all aspects of Soviet society. It alone decided who got important appointments in all aspects of political, economic, and social life; it set the general direction of policy in all areas, leaving it to the lesser (and controlled) bureaucrats of the government bureaucracy to fill in the details; it functioned as the high priesthood of Marxism-Leninism, the infallible doctrine that explained the past and mapped the way toward a communist future; and it maintained surveillance over everything, institutionalized by the presence of party members in key positions and by the more frightening presence of the secret police. Others copied the model, adapting it for local needs or circumstances. Chiang Kai-shek adopted it for the anti-communist Kuomintang in China; Mao adopted it in part for some elements of the Chinese communist revolution, and its role in post-revolutionary China remains constant to this day; the communist regimes created in Eastern Europe after World War II adopted it in the face of Russian dominance; and leaders of anti-colonial independence movements in the third world frequently adopted it as their road map to independence and development.

In some cases, mature post-revolutionary party-state regimes tend to become more pluralistic and to modify their initial revolutionary and modernization doctrines to fit contemporary realities. From the 1960s onward, political rivalries within the Kremlin were increasingly cast in terms of the competition of different economic, institutional, or regional issues. Efforts were made to update the doctrine. Leonid Brezhnev, who ruled from 1964 to 1982, offered "developed socialism" as a model for a mature socialist society, and Mikhail Gorbachev initially sought to transform but not destroy the Soviet system through *perestroika, glasnost,* and *demokratizatsiia.* China also followed the same trajectory, divided between the advocates of different strategies of economic development, different versions of China's role in the world, and competing leadership factions.

Sources of Stability and Instability

The long-term stability of a national ideology regime will be determined by its initial success in bringing about substantial transformations in the nation and its place in the world and by its eventual ability to change from a transformational regime into a stable bureaucratized party-state capable of adaptive reform. At times the goals may seem antithetical, pulling the movement in opposite directions as the regime tries to decide between its initial commitment to social transformation and its long-term needs to restore order and stability to a modernizing nation. Ideology usually plays a dominant role in the early stages of the revolutionary movements. Victory and consolidation of power bring a more prosaic view of the world and the new regime's place in it, and a new set of tasks that require different perspectives and skills.

In the longer perspective, the continuing viability of national ideology regimes lies in their skill in becoming stable governing mechanisms, capable of balancing the need for stability and control while maintaining the perception that the nation still remains "special," endowed with a still legitimate doctrine and on the side of history and "the future," no matter how it may have been redefined over the years. In some fashion, the symbiotic balance between the national and ideological elements of the doctrine must be sustained. It's a difficult balancing act, and one that can quickly collapse, as the failure of communism in the Soviet Union and Eastern Europe demonstrates.

Catastrophic events or other shocks to the system may impact a national ideology regime in different ways. Most such challenges will probably stoke the desire to seek a distinctly national response, even if the fundamental nature of the problem is broader in scope, such as global warming, the environment, or pandemics. Finger-pointing and blaming other nations would probably accompany such parochial responses, especially if the nation in question did not rise well to the occasion. To a lesser degree, ideology might also figure into the response, even though it is framed as a distinctive national variation of a common theme. This is especially true with nations that have deeply identified with a particular process ideology that defines a form of government. Whatever their other differences, nations committed to the creation and maintenance of democratic rule at least express some level of concern with the fate of other democracies, sometimes admittedly limited to lip service but sometimes also manifested in serious diplomatic, economic, or even military support. A similar sense of a common ideologically defined community also existed within the Eastern European communist bloc during the Cold War, sometimes benevolently manifested in mutually supportive diplomatic or economic ties and sometimes more aggressively implemented by Soviet military intervention to "correct" the missteps of bloc members, as in Hungary in 1956 and Czechoslovakia in 1968.

What Would a National Ideology World Look Like?

We've seen what a national ideology would look like, in many different versions. Thankfully brief-lived examples emerged after World War I in the form of German National Socialism and Italian Fascism. Products of failed efforts to create democracies, both initially succeeded in spawning mass movements and charismatic leaders who combined national grievances, economic failure, and a utopian vision of the national future to rise to power. And for a while, they succeeded in their efforts to revitalize what seemed to them to be a failing nation and becoming powerful and disruptive members of the international system.

Other attempts to create national ideology regimes failed primarily because the national and ideological programs never caught on. Arab socialism is one such example. Created to link a new sense of ethnic and cultural identity with socialist ideas in the post–World War II era of national independence, it found its zenith in the creation of the Ba'athist Party in the Levant. Its appeal never spread more broadly throughout the Middle East, largely because it never dealt with more fundamental regional issues such as the impact of Islam, including the divisions between the Sunni and Shia sects, and the resistance of more authoritarian traditional leaders and monarchs.

Efforts to create national ideology regimes were more successful in Russia and China. The 1917 revolution in Russia led to the creation of numerous progressive iterations of what it meant to be a socialist and communist state and to a new sense of national identity vested in the creation of the "soviet people" as a replacement for pre-revolutionary identities. It also spawned the first truly successful iteration of the "party-state," the merger of a transformational party with the traditional bureaucratic mechanisms of the modern state. To be sure, the eventual ossification and stagnation of the state and party apparatus, especially in managing a lagging economy, the growing irrelevance of the dream of a future communist utopia, and the rediscovery of older seductive national identities as Russians, Ukrainians, or Georgians, and so on, brought down the once seemingly unshakable façade of Soviet rule. Mikhail Gorbachev's ill-fated efforts at reforms unleashed an uncontrollable revolution of rising expectations that could never be satisfied. But the lesson is not so much about the self-induced collapse of the system, but about the remarkable fact that it survived for 74 years, 1 month, and 28 days as an example of a national ideology experiment.[11]

China has set itself on the same trajectory. Beginning with a distinctly Chinese version of a socialist revolution, it lurched through a series of economic and social models—Mao's Great Leap Forward from 1958 to 1962, his Cultural Revolution from 1966 to 1976, Deng's creation of a socialist market economy from 1978 to 2012, and Xi's latest version of "socialism with Chinese characteristics" launched in 2012—all offering different but distinctly national versions of a socialist future. Consistent also has been the Chinese model of government control over all aspects of the society, with real power vested into the hands of the Communist Party and strong central leadership, increasingly held by a small group labeled the Standing Committee of the Politburo, the party general secretary, and the president, the latter two positions now firmly held by Xi, who no longer faces a mandatory two-term limit as president.[12]

The Cold War also taught us something about what a future world dominated by national ideology regimes might look like. Both the structure and the dynamics of the international system were dominated by the merger of powerful nation-states with utopian, chiliastic, and transformational ideologies. At times it was a dangerous and toxic mix. Everything was defined by the confrontation of these national ideology regimes. It wasn't just the United States and Europe aligned against the Soviet Union, its Eastern European allies, and China; it was also about the clash of all-defining ideological and socioeconomic systems that struggled for preeminence in military strength, economic achievement, cultural accomplishments, and every four years, Olympic medals. To be sure, the superpowers eventually learned how to manage the standoff through deterrence and diplomacy, but the threat was always in the background. Any future international system defined by the rise of aggressive national ideology regimes could be equally perilous and challenging.

POPULISM BECOMES THE DOMINANT PARADIGM

Paradigms seldom make the headlines in the post–Cold War world. Today there is one recent exception: populism. For some, is it a long-overdue acceptance of our real identity, coupled with a rejection of a political process in which "they" have misled and exploited "us." For others, it is an unsettling challenge to the post–World War II consensus that underpinned liberal democracy, widespread social and economic progress, the growing role of international organizations, and ever-expanding economic and cultural globalization.

Populism takes many possible political and social forms. Its right-wing and conservative manifestations reawaken forgotten or suppressed notions of national, cultural, or religious identity, telling "us" that we are different from "them," and frequently calling forth authoritarian movements and charismatic leaders who can restore the true order of things. Marine Le Pen in France, Viktor Orban in Hungary, Donald Trump in the United States, and the Brexiteers in Great Britain summon their followers back to the future, rebuilding whatever once made them "great." The left-wing and progressive manifestations of populism offer a very different future, built upon the creation of a more egalitarian and pluralistic society, political empowerment, social and economic equality and justice, and an increasingly interwoven international community based on further globalization and interdependence. President Emmanuel Macron in France, political parties like Syriza in Greece and Podemus in Spain, and the increasingly radical and assertive left wing of the Democratic Party in the United States represented by the candidacies of Bernie Sanders or Elizabeth Warren offer a very different future.[13]

Both versions of populism have many things in common. They are deeply transformational and increasingly radical in their aspirations and tactics. They reject centrism, both as an ideological description of their program and as a playbook for winning political power at the polls. They are political movements as much as political parties, and their leaders frequently are, or aspire to be, charismatic and frequently authoritarian figures. As agents of change, they are purposely disruptive, shattering the legal and social norms of political behavior to demonstrate their commitment to change and to attract a broad following of voters disenchanted with the conventional political class. They are rebels who, despite their skepticism of the existing order, are willing to try, perhaps for the last time, to transform it through the ballot box.

Broadly defined, populism is an ideology that "pits a virtuous and homogeneous people against a set of elites and dangerous 'others' who are together depicted as depriving . . . the sovereign people of their rights, values, prosperity, identity, and voice."[14] It's "us"—the people, alike and united—against "them"—those not like us, either by virtue of their elite status or because of something vague and menacing—that makes them the "other." We, the people, are a united community, defined by identity, culture, religion, nationality, or whatever else binds us together; in the terminology of political science, we are not a "pluralistic community," artificially united by transactional associations and an ever-changing social contract, but rather a community of the whole, a tribe unto ourselves. We are "sovereign," all empowered, or at least we should be. "They," on the other hand, are not like us, either because they have risen to power that now sets them apart even though they were once "us," or because they are simply not a part of our tribe. They control and exploit "us," compromising our rights, corrupting our values, commandeering our prosperity, and changing our identity. It's "us" versus "them," in a righteous and all-defining struggle.

As with most ideologies that reduce social and economic struggle to a confrontation between elites and the masses, populism polarizes the struggle into fundamentally opposing camps. One camp—the masses, however defined—is virtuous and deserving, the victims of an otherwise unjust society, an uneven distribution of wealth and opportunity, biased and corrupt political institutions, and willfully exploitive and manipulative political leadership. But united, mobilized, and made conscious of their victimization by enlightened and probably charismatic leaders who can make a substantive and emotional connection with them, the common folk can rise to the occasion and make a difference. The elite, whether essentially a privileged extension of community itself or a different "other," has its role as well, joining the battle in defense of the existing order or seeking to limit conflict through the creation of a stable but artificial political center.

Broadly speaking, two different although sometimes overlapping and mutually supportive explanations have been offered to explain the recent emergence of populist movements. The first, usually called the "cultural backlash model," focuses primarily on the rejection of cosmopolitan and post-material values and social norms associated with the spread of economic and cultural globalization after World War II. Economic integration and interdependence, cultural homogenization, increasing mobility, and global communications have destroyed the distinctiveness of identities, cultures and social norms that once made us uniquely French, or Hungarian, or American. "Us" has expanded to include "them," and we no longer recognize what made "us," well, "us." The melting pot has melted us into a homogeneous amalgam of things we once were and things we never wanted to be.

It's unsettling, not knowing who you are, or not having social and cultural guidelines to tell you where you fit in and how to behave. The tribe has lost its sense of tribal identity and cohesion. Divisions cut across the community in many ways. Economic distinctions create new "haves" and "have-nots," and even more disturbingly, a growing and increasingly angry community of "once but no longer haves." Generational distinctions become more acute and divisive, as do fault lines established by education, urban or rural residence, and personal lifestyle choices. We have lost our sense of cultural identity, and we are not sure why. Perhaps it is the inevitable response to broader social and economic events that no one could control. Or, more ominously, perhaps it is the outcome of conscious intent and manipulation, either by those already among "us" or by "them," the outsiders, seeking to change "us" into "them" or to replace "us" altogether.

The second explanation places greater emphasis on the economic displacement of a once-secure middle class and/or blue-collar working class rooted in a viable industrial base, a prosperous agricultural sector built around the traditional family farm, and a stable retail economy. It was the United States of the 1950s and 1960s, secure and complacent that its prosperity would survive the test of time, and its equivalents in the industrial and commercial economies of Western Europe. It didn't last, a victim of its own aspirations to build a global economy to ensure the prosperity and stability of the West, then perceived as in existential competition with the Soviet empire, an emerging China, and the international communist movement. The creation of free trade areas such as the Common Market, which eventually led to the formation of the European Union, and the success of a series of tariff-lowering agreements brokered by the General Agreement on Tariffs and Trade (GATT, later renamed the World Trade Organization, or WTO) broadened the scope of international trade and deepened economic interdependence. But at the same time, these pacts also set the stage for increasing competition between already-industrialized and emerging industrial nations. Capital, labor, and technology now easily crossed once impermeable borders, both changing the nature of the overall global economy and altering once stable national economies in unanticipated ways. Industrial jobs were "outsourced" to foreign laborers willing to work for less, or the workers themselves migrated into established industrial areas. Investment capital now sought profitable use on a global scale, and advanced technology moved with almost equal ease. While some benefited from the new normal of international trade, others suffered as established industries were forced to adjust by cutting wages, laying off workers, or transferring production abroad.

Like the loss of cultural identity, the loss of economic security stoked the emergence of populist movements. Workers who once regarded themselves as secure for life, with their children likely following in their footsteps, found themselves out of work, lucky to find lower paying and less meaningful employment. Family breadwinners, single parents, or young workers who once envisioned a predictable and secure future now faced an unknown path, at best marked by downward mobility and diminished expectations, and at worst by seeing the bottom drop out below them. Economic change, however beneficial to the global economy as a whole, hollowed out traditional industrial heartlands from the American rust belt to the languishing industrial midlands of central and northern England and Scotland. Someone had done this, or let it happen. Someone had to take the blame. And someone had to do something.

The Structure of a Populism Paradigm

In structural terms, populism usually is a hybrid of a protest movement coupled with a political party and a charismatic and frequently authoritarian leader. It often starts as a relatively small, single-grievance party like the National Front (now the National Rally) in France, first led by Jean-Marie Le Pen, father of the current leader, Marine Le Pen. Initially appealing to a limited political base defined in economic, ethnic, or regional terms, such parties are frequently on the fringes of the political life, usually faring better in parliamentary systems that reward them with a few seats once they cross the cut-off point at the polls. Their initial successes frequently come in local or regional elections, or in the separate elections for the European Parliament, where their success is often a bellwether of growing support at home. Sensing opportunity, they frequently broaden their appeals to attract other disaffected voters and put forward more politically skilled and acceptable candidates. The National Front in France morphed into the more inclusive National Rally, and Marine Le Pen at first marginalized and then expelled her more radical father from the party. In Italy, the Northern League followed a similar trajectory, beginning as a small regional party primarily concerned with local issues and the distinctive grievances of the northern third of the nation, eventually broadening its appeals to other regions and relabeling itself simply the League. It now enjoys widespread national support because of its much broader role in championing regional, economic, and social grievances.

In a somewhat different configuration, populist parties sometimes start out as small factions within a much broader "big tent" party and subsequently capture and transform their more moderate hosts. This is especially likely where such broad political coalitions are deemed necessary to build majority support in a presidential system (the United States is the best example), or where there is no tradition of building post-electoral coalitions based on the support of several smaller but well-defined parties, as in many European multiparty systems. Given the opportunity, the once marginal Eurosceptic wing of the Conservative Party in Great Britain virtually captured the party through capitalizing on the nation's willingness to leave the European Union, eventually spawning a separate Brexit Party when the Tories seemed unwilling or unable to sever ties with Europe. The hardcore pro-Brexit Tories, under the leadership of Boris Johnson, a colorful but marginal Tory who served as the mayor of London, won a decisive victory in the 2019 elections. The same was true with the Tea Party wing of the U.S. Republican Party, which arose because of growing right-wing objections to the party's centrist leadership and its rejection of more conservative positions on social policy and lifestyle issues central to the so-called culture wars. Their successful efforts to pull the party further to the right set the stage for the rise of Donald Trump, whose surprise victory in 2016 was based both on traditional Republican voters and a broad spectrum of angry or disaffected voters responding to a platform of typical populist economic and social grievances.

Populist parties usually score their first victories on simplistic and deeply emotional issues that touch on a sense of victimization, displacement, or marginalization. Our jobs have disappeared, gone "over there" through outsourcing, and to "them," who now live among us. Our sense of shared cultural identity has been "corrupted" or "devalued" by growing social pluralism. Our families and communities are splitting apart, victims of economic necessity, an endangered sense of identity and unity, and a host of other issues such as drug abuse and suicide that followed quickly in their wake. Skillful populist leaders consolidate their leadership and expand their support by reaching out to other disaffected constituencies, creating ever-increasing coalitions of the once neglected, marginalized, and disgruntled voters.

Charismatic and often authoritarian leaders often become an important part of expanding the populist base. Long having turned away from the smooth-talking yet hollow demeanor of the political class, populist voters respond to the tell-it-like-it-is bluntness of charismatic leaders who identify the enemies among us and abroad, talk of conspiracies and plots to mislead or replace us, and offer simple yet reassuring solutions that fit easily on a bumper sticker, in a ten-second sound bite, or on the front of a baseball cap. Such leaders are seen as "tough" and "unconventional," and their willingness to break the rules of conventional political battle energize and delight their supporters. The United States' Donald Trump and Britain's Boris Johnson are masters of the game, with Italy's Matteo Salvini, Hungary's Viktor Orban, or Turkey's Recep Tayyip Erdogan close behind. To be sure, populist leaders are political animals, and their message will be nuanced for different audiences. But the core will remain constant: I am the only leader who can fix things, and I will do whatever it takes.

The emergence of populist parties, or their elevation from the political fringe to center stage often is associated with a particular tipping point, something that crystalizes or redefines an issue, underscores the failure of the existing political class, or shocks a formerly inert disaffected and marginalized voters into action. Economic downturns are a common catalyst, the deeper and more widespread the better. Local or regional impacts are most common, at least a first, but their cumulative impact is far-reaching. Auto factories close, coal mines shut down, the local Sears or Penney's store is shuttered, or the only local small-town grocery store closes its doors—it all seems local at first, until you learn that it is happening all over the country, and all over most of the older industrialized world. The 2008 global economic crisis had similar impact, perhaps even on a broader scale, but its town-by-town, person-by-person consequences were slower to manifest themselves.

Demographic changes also can produce tipping points, usually when the initially unnoticed transformation of the community or the workforce reaches a hard-to-ignore critical mass, or when a new wave of migration and immigration occurs because of economic hardship in other nations or wars and natural disasters that produce a flood of refugees. What had seemed distant and abstract is now close and unavoidably real.

How Power Is Distributed in a Populist-Dominated International System

Power is distributed, or perhaps more accurately, redistributed, since the typical populist playbook is based on far-reaching political change. By its nature, populism is rooted in a rejection of the existing order of things, or at least that is the way it is portrayed by its leaders to the disgruntled "masses," no matter how much they themselves are members of the political class. At the least, the presence of a viable populist movement probably signals significant change in the nature of the party structure; a new or once fringe party has moved into the mainstream, or an existing party has been captured by populists within it. New leaders also have taken the stage, or old ones have adapted their public persona to win broader support. Donald Trump and Boris Johnson are good examples. Long on the fringes of U.S. politics, Trump transformed himself from a political joke to an unanticipated force to be reckoned with by the Republican establishment and the Democratic opposition alike. Johnson, on the other hand, had served as the Conservative Party mayor of London, dramatically altering his strategy by winning a seat in the House of Commons and more closely identifying himself with the Brexit wing of the party.

Formal institutional change within government itself will be more limited, at least as long as new populist leaders can achieve their ends within the existing structure. But given the transformational and charismatic nature of the new leadership itself, real political power will shift toward the executive branch in presidential systems or the prime minister in parliamentary systems. Populist leaders will capitalize on their personalized connection with the voters, who are themselves increasingly cut loose from traditional party or associational ties. The legal or de facto arrangements that had provided checks and balances will be eroded, if not formally abandoned, a not surprising result if we remember that a part of the populist revolt was a reaction to the hyper-partisanship and self-imposed gridlock of the existing political class. A "new normal" will emerge, defined by the personal style of the new populist leaders, the extent to which new and more stable parties emerge, and to the underlying stability of the institutional structure within which they work. Or perhaps it will be a series of "new normals," each defined by new leaders and unstable voting patterns, until some measure of stability returns.

Nations led by populist leaders will tend to be disruptive within the existing international system, altering their foreign policies, trade arrangements, and alliances to suit their vision of their country's best interests and their list of grievances against the outside world. On the whole, they will tend to be less engaged, protecting or purifying their own cultures, resisting immigration, altering their trade patterns to protect or rebuild the domestic economy, and rethinking existing alliance structures or future commitments. Most likely even the most ardent populists will not become outright isolationists, but they will approach the outside world on a more transactional basis, picking and choosing both formal and informal commitments with a wary concern for the costs as well as the benefits.

In all likelihood, it will take some time for populist nations to define their role in the international system. It will be determined in part by the permanence of the populist revolution itself. It is uncertain whether the initial wave of populist leaders will consolidate their positions and establish viable political parties or broader institutionalized social movements, or whether they will quickly fade at the polls, either because of the growth of other and perhaps more extreme elements or because the old political establishment reasserts control. Or will the voters eventually tire of populist leaders who promise more than they can deliver? The complexity and intractability of the issues also will play a role; complex economic, social, and cultural issues will defy simple solutions even in the hands of charismatic leaders who have stirred public discontent.

Sources of Stability and Instability

By definition, populism initially entails creating a higher level of political instability within the existing political order. Populist grievances become the wedge issues that pry apart existing political parties and disrupt the smooth operation of the system. But once in power, can they create a new, albeit rebuilt and reimaged, political order? That will depend on a number of things, not all of which are controlled by the first wave of populist leaders. Most important will be the continuing relevance of the goals and issues that animated the first populist revolt. Cultural or economic issues are probably deeply rooted, but they also have their day-to-day manifestations, and leaders must be quick to respond to shifting public opinion or efforts from other wannabe leaders who would redefine the issue of the moment in their favor. Being a charismatic leader may also be difficult to sustain over time; yesterday's visionary rebel becomes today's established leader, old news in the rapidly changing world of public attention and, most dangerously, now the person who can be blamed for whatever problems or failures top today's headlines. The initial success of populism as a political strategy will not be ignored; it will be studied, adapted, and tried, both at home and abroad.

Re-institutionalization may bring a degree of stability, especially if the formal institutions of government have not been fundamentally altered; Congress is still Congress, and Commons still Commons, but now different in a populist world. Rebuilding a stable party system also contributes to enhanced stability, especially if the once disorganized populist movement can build a stable party base, complete with a loyal following, an established role within the legislative and executive branches, and a local presence at the grassroots level. But that will take time, and the more power the organization has, the greater its ability to challenge the independence of its charismatic leader.

Long-term instability also is possible, perhaps in continuing institutional gridlock and the inability of any government to deal with the nation's problems to the satisfaction of increasingly disaffected voters. A wave of increasingly radical and perhaps authoritarian populist revolts could occur, each headed by a new populist leader and spinning the government's failures and his or her new version of populism in more radical tones.

The impact of catastrophic events or other shocks to the system would primarily be determined by how they translated into wedge issues that disrupted (or further disrupted) the political order. At their core, populist revolts are based on the perception of the failure of the existing political order; *they*, and the institutions through which they govern, have failed *us*, the common people. What better proof than a list of new failures to be added to the old? *They* failed to anticipate the impact of global warming or environmental degradation, or to handle an influx of new immigrants, or to staunch a rapidly spreading pandemic, or to . . . The list goes on, probably including both real and imagined (or just exaggerated) threats. But they are the stuff of political manipulation, of playing the next round of populist politics, and of conveying power to the political activists who best exploit them.

WHAT WOULD A POPULIST WORLD LOOK LIKE?

What would a populist world look like? We don't have to look far for the answer, although it's still very much a work in progress and the outcome is uncertain. In many nations, the growing backlash against the post-Cold War world order has taken populist form. Criticism of the effects of economic and cultural globalization and the rediscovery of national identity have resulted in efforts to redefine the world in terms of elite versus mass conflicts on a national and global scale and to reassert the political and cultural significance of a once-waning sense national or communal identity. Exceptionalism—the idea that "we" are inherently different and implicitly superior to "them"—is again center stage, reshaping the nature of domestic politics and challenging once-accepted multinational political, economic, and military commitments.

The impact of populist thinking has so far been, and may continue to be, profoundly transformational at all levels. Some analysts argue that populism's more authoritarian forms may signal the abandonment of Western liberal or pluralistic democracy as we know it, while others aver that it is simply a different institutional form of still essentially democratic rule, a sort of plebiscitary democracy in which voters are content to vest exceptional power into the hands of elected charismatic leaders who offer solutions to their problems. Such populism is equally transformational at the international level, creating a new assortment of revisionist nations that, internally transformed, now set out to change the world around them. Great Britain has left the European Union, and probably will soon have to deal with renewed efforts by Scotland and perhaps others to leave the United Kingdom. In the United States, Donald Trump has reshaped domestic political life and de facto taken control of the Republican Party, and his foreign policy has altered U.S. commitments to trade, defense, and other issues such as global warming and climate change. On the other side of the aisle, the Democratic Party is deeply divided on whether it should remain center-left or endorse more radical and populist themes. In France, the growing popularity of the National Rally under Marine Le Pen and the creation of the new center-left party En Marche, and the presidential victory of Emmanuel Macron have transformed the traditional partisan alignments of the post-Gaullist era, and in Italy similar developments with the growing power of the League have had the same impact. Hungary, Poland, Turkey, and Greece experiment with their own homegrown versions.

To be sure, there are many different and occasionally contradictory elements in these various manifestations of populism. Some tilt to the right, especially on cultural issues and questions of national identity and their exceptional place in the world. Others tilt to the left, especially on economic issues when conflict is defined in terms of the distribution of wealth or opportunity at home and abroad. The style of leadership also differs. Some tilt toward authoritarian populism in which strong charismatic, although usually democratically elected, leaders take control, frequently strengthening the hand of the executive branch against its critics. Others stress greater involvement of excluded or marginalized voters, often favoring a grassroots democratic revolt against the establishment parties of left and right and the "deep state" institutionalized within the government apparatus. As works still in progress, populist leaders and movements may significantly transform politics within some nations and the international system within which they operate. But then again, they may not, especially if their leaders and parties fail to deal with the real-world issues that initially spawned their creation, leaving once hopeful voters adrift once again.

Whatever their substantive or tactical choices, populist movements are purposefully disruptive, at least as viewed by the existing political order. That, indeed, is their purpose and, in the short run, their best strategy. Realigning party structures; redrawing the fault lines of economic, social, and eventually international conflict; reawakening a sense of cultural or economic identity; reanimating potential voters who had abandoned the existing parties; reminding us of who is responsible for our decline and victimization; and refining and endlessly repeating the dual images of what we once were and what we could again be—all are a part of the playbook for a populist transformation of nations and the international system in which they function.

NOTES

1. Andrew Heywood, *Political Ideologies: An Introduction*, 6th ed. (Red Globe, 2017); Michael Freeden, L. T. Sargent, and Marc Stears, eds., *The Oxford Handbook of Ideologies* (Oxford University Press, 2015).

2. http://www.Lexico.com.

3. *Merriam-Webster's Dictionary*, http://www.merriam-webster.com/dictionary/ideology.

4. Rodney Barker, *Political Legitimacy and the State* (Clarendon, 1990); Benno Netelenbos, *Political Legitimacy beyond Weber* (Palgrave Macmillan, 2016); Fabienne Peter, *Democratic Legitimacy* (Routledge, 2009).

5. Patricia Baylis, John Smith, and Steve Owens, *Globalization of World Politics: An Introduction to International Relations* (Oxford University Press, 2017).

6. Tamar Gutner, *International Organizations in World Politics* (CQ, 2016); Michael Barnett and Martha Finnemore, *Rules for the World: International Organizations in World*

Politics (Cornell University Press, 2004); Cecilla Jacob and Martin Mennecke, *Implementing the Responsibility to Protect: A Future Agenda* (Routledge, 2019); Thomas Davies, *NGOs: A New History of Transnational Civil Society* (Oxford University Press, 2014); Monica Serrano and Thomas G. Weiss, *The International Politics of Human Rights: Rally to the R2P Cause* (Routledge, 2014).

7. Daniel J. Hopkins and John Sides, *Political Polarization in American Politics* (Bloomsbury, 2015); Steven E. Schier and Todd E. Eberly, *Polarized: The Rise of Ideology in American Politics* (Rowman & Littlefield, 2016).

8. Andrew Gimson, *Boris: The Making of a Prime Minister* (Simon and Schuster UK, 2019); Kevin O'Rourke, *A Short History of BREXIT: From Brentry to Backstop* (Pelican, 2019); Tim Shipman, *All Our War: The Full Story of How Brexit Sank Britain's Political Class* (William Collins, 2016).

9. Sophie Pedder, *Revolution Francaise: Emmanuel Macron and the Quest to Reinvent a Nation* (Bloomsbury, 2018); Emmanuel Macron, *Revolution* (Scribe US, 2017); Jocelyn Evans and Gilles Ivaldi, *The 2017 French Presidential Election: A Political Reformation?* (Palgrave Macmillan, 2017).

10. Matthew Qvortrup, *Angela Merkel: Europe's Most Influential Leader*, rev. ed. (Abrams, 2017); Stefan Kornelius, *Angela Merkel: The Chancellor and Her World* (Alma, 2014).

11. Alfred Meyer, *Leninism* (Harvard University Press, 1957); Bertram Wolfe, *Three Who Made a Revolution: A Biographical History of Lenin, Trotsky, and Stalin* (Delta, 1964); Theodore von Laue, *Why Lenin? Why Stalin? Why Gorbachev? The Rise and Fall of the Soviet System* (HarperCollins, 1997); Donald R. Kelley, *Russian Politics and Presidential Power: Transformational Leadership from Gorbachev to Putin* (CQ/SAGE, 2016).

12. Marie-Claire Bergere, *Sun Yat-sen* (Stanford University Press, 2000); Tjio Kayloe, *The Unfinished Revolution: Sun Yatsen and the Struggle for Modern China* (Marshall Cavendish, 2018); Maurice Meisner, *Mao Zedong: A Political and Intellectual Portrait* (Polity, 2006); Frank Dikotter, *Cultural Revolution* (Bloomsbury, 2017); Ezra F. Vogel, *Deng Xiaoping and the Transformation of China* (Belnap, 2013); Elizabeth C. Economy, *The Third Revolution: Xi Jinping and the New Chinese State* (Oxford University Press, 2018).

13. John B. Judis, *The Populist Explosion: How the Great Recession Transformed American and European Politics* (Columbia Global Reports, 2016); Roger Eatwell, *National Populism: The Revolt against Liberal Democracy* (Penguin Random House, 2018).

14. Danieli Albertazzi and Duncan McDonnell, eds., *Twenty-First Century Populism* (Palgrave Macmillan, 2008), 3.

6

Where Do You Go from Here?

WHAT HAVE YOU LEARNED?

This book has two purposes. The first is to teach you something about international relations and the complex world in which we live, making it very much like all of the other books that deal with the topic. The second purpose—and really the more important one—is to teach you something about how we think about international relations. To that end, it takes a somewhat unique but, hopefully, helpful approach of not emphasizing the conventional theoretical categories of realism, liberalism, and constructivism, and all of their offshoots. Instead, it asks you to think in terms of *paradigms*, which hopefully by now you understand as fundamentally different ways of understanding the world around us.

Let's remember what paradigms do. They structure the ways in which we define the world around us, telling us what the most important factors are (*variables*, if you want to be methodologically correct), how they interact, and how they shape our broader perception of the world and how we interact with it. At their best, they create an intellectual comfort zone within which we operate, a level of confidence that we've got things figured out. At their worst, they may be completely wrong and factually inaccurate, leading us down the wrong road because they simply don't correspond to reality. In most cases, they are a little of both, giving us a sense that we probably have things figured out, accompanied by the gnawing realization that there are alternative paradigms and explanations that others believe in as fervently as we do in ours.

Ask yourself a question: in terms of the paradigms used in this study, how would you define your perception of the international system? Do you mostly accept the paradigm that stresses the continuing importance of the Westphalian nation-state? Or is economics more important, and if so, which of the many different economic paradigms? Capitalism? Socialism? Some combination of both? If you think the identity and culture paradigm is most important in defining your views, you have the same problem. Which identity or culture? The ideology paradigm also confronts you with the same problem. Which ideology? And in the real world, you probably will have to admit that you accept some combination of elements from different paradigms.

The paradigms also help you to understand the actions of others. They too view the world through the lens of the paradigms that seem most accurate to them. And like you, they probably draw upon multiple paradigms, arranging the elements to suit their own view of the world.

HOW MANY ALTERNATE FUTURES HAVE WE CREATED?

On the face of it, we have created a number of possible futures for the international system. Each starts with one of our basic paradigms—the nation-state, economics, identity and culture, or ideology—and extrapolates many different ways forward that might exist. Some of the alternative futures emerge from just following the basic premises of the paradigm to their logical conclusions. Others come from the interaction of two or more different paradigms. All are basically the sort of "thought experiments" we've described above—intellectual exercises in which we create a picture of a possible future and how it would work and then look at history or the contemporary world to see if we can find an example. Sometimes we do, and sometimes we don't. History shows us examples of a hegemonic system dominated by the major superpower of its day. The

Roman Empire serves as a good example from ancient history, and the brief-lived dominance of the United States for a decade or so just after the end of the Cold War shows us a more recent example. But today's conventional wisdom tells us that a global hegemon is unlikely to emerge in the foreseeable future. Some variation of a multipolar world is more likely, but we're uncertain about how many major players would be involved, how they would interact among themselves or with lesser powers, and how stable such a multipolar configuration would be in the long run. But at least we've got something to work with, a framework built around an initial paradigm (the nation-state, in this case) and how we've spun out its possible incarnations in today's world. Each of the other possible futures is the product of a similar thought experiment, combining the logical extrapolation of our paradigms and an educated guess about whether it is likely to emerge.

Let's quickly review how many possible futures we've created. From the Nation-State Paradigm:

- a hegemonic world, probably unlikely in the near future because of the competition of possible global hegemons like China and the United States, although lesser powers may seek regional hegemony;

- a new balance of power, operating within a bipolar or limited multipolar world, possible if a small number of major powers are checked in their search for hegemony and accept de facto limitations as an acceptable price for the potential stability inherent in a bipolar or limited multipolar standoff;

- a stable multipolar world, made possible by a more widespread distribution of economic and military power and the acceptance of formal and informal restraints by first- and second-tier nations motivated by the desire to avoid or mitigate conflict;

- an unstable multipolar world, rooted in the likely proliferation of military and economic power among many states, the failure of formal institutions and/or informal mechanisms to mitigate conflict, and the impact of failed or rogue states.

From the Economic Paradigm:

- continued globalization, perhaps possible on a limited basis but likely slowed by diminishing returns on past accomplishments and growing economic and political pushback against multilateral institutional mechanisms and globalization's economic and social impact;

- globalization continues in limited form, but amended and reconfigured, increasingly likely in today's world as challenges mount to the World Trade Organization and other multilateral organizations, the European Union, and other multilateral bodies, including regional trade blocs such as NAFTA, now the USMCA;

- mercantilism 2.0, an increasingly popular hybrid of the nation-state and economic paradigms, producing increasingly strident economic nationalism, a transactional and my-country-first approach to trade, and greater reliance on bilateral trade agreements;

- toward autarky, with a touch of anarchy, a worst-case scenario evident in isolated but sometimes still significant efforts to fundamentally reconfigure a nation's place in the global economy, accompanied by extensive political and social changes, as seen in Brexit.

From the Identity and Culture Paradigm:

- the gradual emergence of a global identity and culture, currently present in the world's most prosperous states deeply involved in globalization and international trade, and especially in global cities such as New York or London, but unlikely to spread to less affluent venues;

- the emergence of an increasingly popular and assertive hybrid of the identity and culture paradigm with the nation-state paradigm, providing an institutional base for the rediscovery and assertion of distinct national or subnational identities and cultures that stoke in-group–out-group distinctions and conflicts;

- the "clash of civilizations" paradigm, a once popular but now questioned perspective that fundamental issues of identity and culture will become the primary fault lines of the international system, pushing aside the more institutionalized features of the nation-state paradigm and the class- or wealth-related distinctions of the economic paradigm.

From the Ideology Paradigm:

- the gradual emergence of a universalistic and humanistic ideology, undercutting previous ideological fault lines, and closely aligned with the simultaneous emergence of a global identity and culture, currently present in nascent form in more advanced, affluent, and cosmopolitan nations and global cities;

- the reemergence of past ideological conflicts in a new form, resulting either from the redefinition and reanimation of the traditional notions of "left" or "right" or from a resurgence of the debate over political legitimacy and the various social processes, such as democracy or authoritarianism, through which it can be established;

- the emergence of "national ideology," a hybrid of the nation-state and ideological paradigms, producing a fusion of ideology and national identity to justify an idiosyncratic national version of a broader ideological perspective such as Stalin's "socialism in one country" or Xi Jinping's "socialism with Chinese characteristics";

- the growing assertion of populism as a fusion of the nation-state, identity and culture, and ideological paradigms that justifies the defense of the traditional nation-state and its unique sense of identity and culture, combined with a redefinition of the internal political struggles in terms of broader elite-mass, rather than traditional, economic or social, fault lines.

The first thing to notice is the complexity of the many possibilities. Some emerge directly from the nature of the core paradigm. The nation-state paradigm produces possible futures that offer sometimes radically different possibilities based on the continuing centrality of nation-states; the economic paradigm follows the same logic, but produces very different possible future international systems; and the same patterns emerge for the identity/culture and ideology paradigms. No surprises there, except to perhaps marvel at the different future trajectories that may flow from the same starting point.

Even greater complexity emerges when paradigms begin to merge, resulting in hybrid futures based on the interaction of different paradigms. The merger of the nation-state and economic paradigms produces the mercantilism 2.0 hybrid based on economic nationalism and extensive revisions of the once-dominant globalization model. The merger of the nation-state and identity and culture paradigms gives rise to a hybrid based on the close identification between issues of identity and culture as manifested in the mechanism of the traditional nation-state. In the same vein, the merger of the nation-state and ideology paradigms produces the national ideology variation, while the three-way merger of the nation-state, identity and culture, and ideological paradigms gives us some variation of populism.

The nature of any future international system is further complicated by the reality that no one paradigm will ever be universally accepted by every member of the international system. We'll just never agree on one simple basic truth that works for all of us. Powerful nations will most likely be inclined toward a hegemonic, bipolar, or limited multipolar world view; economically powerful nations will be focused on some variation of the economic paradigm; and identity and culture or ideology will be the core of the worldview of nations or non-state actors who regard either one as the centerpiece of their paradigm. We always have, and will continue to, live in a world of competing paradigms that define and motivate us. The best we can do is to try to understand the others' way of looking at the world and, perhaps just as importantly, to understand what makes us tick.

HOW CAN YOU USE THIS FRAMEWORK?

Thought Experiment 1—What Are You?
Let's try a *thought experiment*, which is an intellectual exercise in which we try to apply a particular paradigm to see what it tells us about reality. Which paradigm(s) define you? Begin with the most important thing that shapes how you view the world and defines your place within it. Is your national identity the starting point? If so, how much does it fill in the blanks in suggesting the other parts of your worldview? Being an American, or any other nationality, is in part a legal identity; you are the citizen of a particular nation-state, by birth or naturalization, and you have the birth certificate or naturalization papers to prove it. You may even have simultaneous citizenship in several nations. But how much does that citizenship mean to you? Does being a citizen of a particular country also convey a sense of ethnic or cultural identity? Or an economic or ideological identity? For some people, the answer will be yes, revealing that in many cases, paradigms are linked in mutually supportive packages or clusters, each feature implying the others. But in other cases, there may be no obvious connections, leaving you either defined by a single paradigmatic identity, or compelling you to come up with your own unique combination.

What if some other paradigm lies at the core of your identity? If the economic paradigm is the bedrock of your personal paradigm, you'll understand and engage the world from that perspective: as a blue- or white-collar worker, a member of the proletariat or capitalist class, a capitalist or socialist, or a member of the elite "one percent" as opposed to the other "ninety-nine percent," depending on how you perceive your own economic role. Elements of the other paradigms will probably be there—citizenship in a particular nation-state, or culture, or ideology—but as less significant, but probably supportive, parts of the big picture. But you won't see the world in quite the same way as a person who puts citizenship in a particular nation-state, or identity and culture, or ideology at the head of the list. If identity and culture or ideology is the core of your worldview, the mix will be different, with citizenship or economics playing a reduced role, or perhaps no significant role.

Thought Experiment 2—Understanding Our Leaders

Now that you've gotten the hang of thinking in terms of thought experiments, let's try another one. In this case, choose a political leader, past or present. It could be a U.S. president, a British prime minister, a Russian president or Communist Party leader, a Chinese leader, or the leader of your own country if we've not mentioned him or her. Anybody. Now ask yourself which paradigm most characterizes his or her view of the world. Picking the dominant paradigm will be easy, or so it seems at first. Each is the leader of a Westphalian nation-state, so being the American, or French, or British leader cannot be far from their minds. But how much does it tell you? Are they a "my country first and foremost" sort of nationalist, or a "my country as a participant in a multinational or multipolar world in which each nation's interests must be acknowledged" sort of nationalist? It will make a difference. At the time of this writing, the United States' Donald Trump, Britain's Boris Johnson, and Russia's Vladimir Putin would mostly fit into the former category, while Germany's Angela Merkel and France's Emmanuel Macron would mostly fall into the latter. But the qualifying "mostly" is always necessary; no leader, even the most seemingly single-minded, will be that consistent in his or her views.

That brings us to a new level of complexity: nobody can be completely understood in terms of a single paradigm. People are not that simple, and their views of the world will be inherently complex. Is the leader you chose really that simple? Or do other paradigms also enter into the picture? Someone whom we acknowledge as "mostly" a nationalist will also be affected by other paradigms. Donald Trump or Boris Johnson certainly fit most easily into the paradigm that stresses a nation-state–defined world. It's probably the most important core element of their view of the world. But both are also shaped by their own distinctive views of economics and their sense of identity and culture. All of these elements somehow combine to create the bigger picture, the complex and multifaceted paradigm that each carries around in his or her head.

Thought Experiment 3—Explain the Headlines

A final experiment: choose a particular headline from today's news. Something important, or perhaps just something that catches your eye. It can be a particular event—Brexit, the outcome of an election somewhere in the world, an ongoing war like that in Afghanistan, or an act of terrorism—anything. Try to explain that event and the its background in terms of our paradigms. Was Brexit about interpreting what being a sovereign nation-state means in the twenty-first century? Or about Britain's domestic economy and its place in the global economy? Or about its sense of identity and culture? Or, finally, about some ideologically inspired sense of what "democracy" means? The answer, of course, is all of the above, although you'll get a spirited argument about which is more important. And the answer will also depend upon whom you ask. To the eurosceptic faction of the Conservative Party, it's always about the defense of British sovereignty against the invasive presence of the European Union and its regulations and bureaucrats. To the now unemployed factory workers of the hollowed-out north and midlands, it's primarily about economics. To both, despite their differences, it's also about a sense of identity and culture now challenged by migrant workers and immigrants and by the cosmopolitan elites that dominate a global city like London. And to many, it's more fundamentally about the kind of leaders they choose, ranging from the ranks of the long-established parties like the Conservatives and Labour, or unconventional candidates like Boris Johnson, whose populist and unconventional style lets him capture control of the nation's oldest and most successful party and turn it to his purpose. You'll probably conclude that each of the paradigms has something relevant to say, although some seem to be more important than others.

So Where Does That Leave You?

"Confused" may be your first answer, and that's understandable. If you are reading this book in connection with a course on international relations or contemporary history, you are being exposed to an enormous complexity of events, theories, and possible explanations, many of which say completely opposite things. But that's normal, at least in an open debate about how we understand and explain what's happening in the world around us. But remember that we view that world through different lenses that determine what we see. Understanding how our perceptions are shaped by those lenses, which we've called "paradigms," is the first but not the only step to figuring it out.

Index

About the Author

Donald R. Kelley is professor of political science at the University of Arkansas, Fayetteville, where he has taught since 1980.

His publications on Russia include *The Economic Superpowers and the Environment: The United States, the Soviet Union, and Japan*, coauthor, 1976; *Soviet Politics in the Brezhnev Era*, editor, 1980; *The Solzhenitsyn-Sakharov Dialogue: Politics, Society, and the Future*, 1982; *The Politics of Developed Socialism*, 1986; *Soviet Politics from Brezhnev to Gorbachev*, editor, 1987; *Old Myths and New Realities in United States–Soviet Relations*, coeditor, 1990; *Perestroika Era Politics: The New Soviet Legislature and Gorbachev's Political Reforms*, coeditor, 1991; *The Sons of Sergei: Khrushchev and Gorbachev as Reformers*, coeditor, 1992; *Politics in Russia and the Successor States*, 1999; *After Communism: Perspectives on Democracy*, editor, 2003; and *Russian Politics and Presidential Power: Transformational Leadership from Gorbachev to Putin*, 2017.

Other books include *The Clinton Riddle*, coeditor, 2004; *Divided Power: The Presidency, Congress, and the Formation of American Foreign Policy*, editor, 2005; and *Taking the Measure: The Presidency of George W. Bush*, coeditor, 2013.

He is currently at work on a book on Russian politics from the 2012 to the 2024 presidential elections.